White Coat,

By the same author

Poetry
Walking Under Water
Tenants of the House
Poems, Golders Green
A Small Desperation
Funland and Other Poems
Collected Poems 1948–1976
Way Out in the Centre
Ask the Bloody Horse

Plays
House of Cowards
The Dogs of Pavlov
Pythagoras (Smith)

Novels
Ash on a Young Man's Sleeve
Some Corner of an English Field
O. Jones, O. Jones

Other Prose
A Poet in the Family(Autobiography)
A Strong Dose of Myself (Confessions, Stories, Essays)
Journals from the Ant-Heap

White Coat, Purple Coat

Collected Poems 1948–1988

Dannie Abse

HUTCHINSON
London Sydney Auckland Johannesburg

Collected Poems 1948–1976 first published in 1977
Revised and extended edition entitled *White Coat, Purple Coat Collected Poems 1948–1988* first published in Great Britain in 1989 by Century Hutchinson Ltd,
Brookmount House, 62–65 Chandos Place, Covent Garden, London WC2N 4NW

Century Hutchinson Publishing Group (Australia) Pty Ltd
89–91 Albion Street, Surry Hills, NSW 2010

Century Hutchinson (NZ) Ltd
32–34 View Road, PO Box 40-086, Glenfield, Auckland 10

Century Hutchinson Group (SA) Pty Ltd
PO Box 337, Bergvlei 2012, South Africa

Set by Rowland Phototypesetting Ltd
Bury St Edmunds, Suffolk
Printed and bound in Great Britain by
Anchor Brendon Ltd
Tiptree, Essex

British Library Cataloguing in Publication Data
Abse, Dannie, *1923–*
White coat, purple coat: collected poems, 1948–1988.
I. Title
821'.914

ISBN 0 09 172644 1

I should like to take this opportunity to thank Giles Gordon of Anthony Sheil Associates Ltd, and Tony Whittome of Century Hutchinson for their unswerving concern for my work and their supportive friendship over many years.

White Coat, Purple Coat is dedicated to my wife, Joan.

D.A.

Contents

White Coat, Purple Coat

Collected Poems 1948–1988

Dannie Abse

The uninvited

They came into our lives unasked for.
There was light momentarily, a flicker of wings,
a dance, a voice, and then they went out
again, like a light, leaving us not so much
in darkness, but in a different place
and alone as never before.

So we have been changed
and our vision no longer what it was,
and our hopes no longer what they were;
so a piece of us has gone out with them also,
a cold dream subtracted without malice,

the weight of another world added also,
and we did not ask, we did not ask ever
for those who stood smiling
and with flowers before the open door.

We did not beckon them in, they came in uninvited,
the sunset pouring from their shoulders,
so they walked through us as they would through
 water,
and we are here, in a different place,
changed and incredibly alone,
and we did not know, we do not know ever.

Epithalamion

Singing, today I married my white girl
beautiful in a barley field.
Green on thy finger a grass blade curled,
so with this ring I thee wed, I thee wed,
and send our love to the loveless world
of all the living and all the dead.

Now, no more than vulnerable human,
we, more than one, less than two,
are nearly ourselves in a barley field –
and only love is the rent that's due
though the bailiffs of time return anew
to all the living but not the dead.

Shipwrecked, the sun sinks down harbours
of a sky, unloads its liquid cargoes
of marigolds, and I and my white girl
lie still in the barley – who else wishes
to speak, what more can be said
by all the living against all the dead?

Come then all you wedding guests:
green ghost of trees, gold of barley,
you blackbird priests in the field,
you wind that shakes the pansy head
fluttering on a stalk like a butterfly;
come the living and come the dead.

Listen flowers, birds, winds, worlds,
tell all today that I married
more than a white girl in the barley –
for today I took to my human bed
flower and bird and wind and world,
and all the living and all the dead.

Song for Dov Shamir

Working is another way of praying.
You plant in Israel the soul of a tree.
You plant in the desert the spirit of gardens.

Praying is another way of singing.
You plant in the tree the soul of lemons.
You plant in the gardens the spirit of roses.

Singing is another way of loving.
You plant in the lemons the spirit of your son.
You plant in the roses the soul of your daughter.

Loving is another way of living.
You plant in your daughter the spirit of Israel.
You plant in your son the soul of the desert.

Letter to Alex Comfort

Alex, perhaps a colour of which neither of us had dreamt
may appear in the test-tube with God knows what
    admonition.
Ehrlich, certainly, was one who broke down the mental
    doors,
yet only after his six hundred and sixth attempt.

Koch also, painfully, and with true German thoroughness,
eliminated the impossible to prove that too many of us
are dying from the same disease. Visible, on the slide
at last – Death – and the thin bacilli of an ancient distress.

Still I, myself, don't like Germans, but prefer the unkempt
voyagers who, like butterflies drunk with suns,
can only totter crookedly in the dazed air
to reach, charmingly, their destination as if by accident.

That Greek one, then, is my hero who watched the bath
    water
rise above his navel, and rushed out naked, 'I found it,
I found it' into the street in all his shining and forgot
that others would only stare at his genitals.
    What laughter!

Or Newton, leaning in Woolsthorpe against the garden wall,
forgot his indigestion and all such trivialities,
but gaped up at heaven in just surprise, and, with
true gravity, witnessed the vertical apple fall.

O what a marvellous observation! Who would have
  reckoned
that such a pedestrian miracle could alter history,
that, henceforward, everyone must fall, whatever
their rank, at thirty-two feet per second, per second?

You too, I know, have waited for doors to fly open, played
with your cold chemicals, written long letters
to the Press; listened to the truth afraid, and dug deep
into the wriggling earth for a rainbow with an honest spade.

But nothing rises. Neither spectres, nor oil, nor love.
And the old professor must think you mad, Alex, as you
  rehearse
poems in the laboratory like vows, and curse those clever
  scientists
who dissect away the wings and haggard heart from the
  dove.

Portrait of a marriage

To the suburban house you return again
with a new hat and the stammering discourse
of mild rebellion. You dare not entertain
questions like – Can I start again? Seek divorce?
Because now, middle-aged, you would gain
nothing but insecurity and remorse,
all the might-have-beens crying in the brain.

It was false even before the first caress
but how you strove to make it true,
fouling silence, talking louder to suppress
the lie that somehow grew and grew,
as you hid each new distress
behind the photograph of the smile and you
less than radiant in your wedding dress.

And, in the stabbed evenings, when the sun
died, by appointment, in its Joseph's coat,
you asked help from that anyone
whose million edition pen could write
romantic novels to overcome
the truth of the lonely all about,
the taste of nothing on your tongue.

Now, one year's gone since your clumsy honeymoon
and he talks to you behind an unlocked door;
again your artificial smile alone
floats between the ceiling and the floor,
like some quiet heartbreak, almost to condone
what, after all, others too must slow endure,
the clock, the unhappiness, the civilized bore.

Until those untamed voices in this tidy room
weirdly rise again to show
what is your and your husband's doom,
the dullness you should never know,
the silent piano in the gloom,
the cut-glass vases you endow
with flowers, to disguise this here and now.

Albert

Albert loved dogs mostly, though this was absurd
for they always slouched away when he touched their
  fur,
but once, perching on his shoulder, alighted a bird;

a bird alive as fire and magical as that day
when clear-eyed Héloïse met Peter Abelard.
Though cats followed him, the bird never flew away.

And dogs pursued the cats which hunted the bird.
Albert loved dogs deeply but was jealously hurt
that they pursued him merely because of the bird;

the bird alive as fire and magical as that day.
So one morning he rose and murdered the bird.
But then the cats vanished and the dogs went away.

Albert hated dogs after, though this was absurd.

The mountaineers

Despite the drums we were ready to go.
The natives warned us shaking their spears.
Soon we'd look down on them a mile below
rather as Icarus, so many poets ago,
waved to those shy, forlorn ones, dumb on a thumbnail field.
We started easily but oh the climb was slow.

Above us, the grey perilous rocks like our pride
rose higher and higher – broken teeth of the mountain –
while below the dizzy cliffs, the tipsy angles signified
breathless vertigo and falling possible suicide.
So we climbed on, roped together. At the night camps
our voices babel yet our journey glorified.

The soul too has altitudes and the great birds fly
over. All the summer long we climbed higher,
crag above crag under a copper sulphate sky,
peak above peak singing of the deserted, shy,
inconsolable ones. Still we climb to the chandelier stars
and the more we sing the more we die.

So ascending in that high Sinai of the air,
in space and canyons of the spirit, we lost ourselves
amongst the animals of the mountain – the terrible stare
of self meeting itself – and no one would dare
return, descend to that most flat and average world.
Rather, we made a small faith out of a tall despair.

Shakespeare, Milton, Wordsworth, came this way
near the lonely precipice, their faces gold
in the marigold sunset. But they could never stay
under the hurricane tree so climbed to allay
that voice which cried: 'You may never climb again.'
Our faces too are gold but our feet are clay.

We discovered more than footprints in the snow,
more than mountain ghost, more than desolate glory,
yet now, looking down, we see nothing below
except wind, steaming ice, floating mist – and so
silently, sadly, we follow higher the rare songs of oxygen.
The more we climb the further we have to go.

Letter to *The Times*

Sir, I have various complaints to make.
The roses, first. When they are ripped
from the earth expiring, we sigh for them,
prescribe tap-water, aspirin, and salt.
But when we lie down under the same earth,
in a dry silly box, do they revive us?
Their odour of rose-ghosts does not change
at all, and they continue to call out
in their red and white morse the old, old
messages as if nothing had happened. Again,
consider trees. My God, the impresario
trees. Just try, Sir, just try to cut one down
in Fitzjohn's Avenue at three o'clock
in the ordinary afternoon. You will be
prosecuted. Soon the Householders will arrange
themselves into a deranged *mob*. They'll grow
Hitler moustaches, Mussolini chins. Frightful,
and write oathy letters to the Council,
naming you *tree-criminal*. Yet tell me, when

the bombs met their shadows in London,
amidst the ruins of voices, did one tree, just one
tree write an angry note in its sly green ink?
No, they only dropped faded tears in autumn
selfishly thinking of their own hamadryads . . .
BUSINESS AS USUAL was, and is, their trite
slogan. Away then with trees and roses.
They are inhuman. Away also with rivers:
the disgusting Ganges bleeding from Brahma's
big toe; the Rubicon cause of a Civil War;
the Acheron, River of Sorrows; Tiber that drowned
Horatius the One-Eyed; the sweating Rhône,
Rhine, Don, and the vulgar Volga, not to
mention the garrulous Mississippi with its
blatant river-smell. Even the English
rivers can do no more than reflect inverted
values, turn chaste swans upside down
like so many flies on the roof of the waters.
Swans, however, *cannot* swim upside down.
At least, I have never seen them. Is this distortion
of truth deliberate? Has ever one river,
one river, Sir, written eulogies of waterfalls
to plead for the reprieve of Mankind? And stars,
so indifferent and delinquent, stars which we have
decorated with glittering adjectives more numerous
than those bestowed on Helen's eyes – do they
warn us when they fall? Not a hint.
Not a star-wink. They are even too lazy
to shine when we are most awake. Creatures
of night, they are probably up to immoral
purposes. You can't trust a star, that's sure.

So when the greenfly is in the rose,
and the dragonfly drops its shadow in the river;
when the axe hides in the tree with its listening
shriek, and clouds gag the starlight
with grey handkerchiefs – I contend, Sir,
that we should pity them no more,
but concern ourselves with more natural things.

Duality

Twice upon a time,
there was a man who had two faces,
two faces but one profile:
not Jekyll and Hyde, not good and bad,
and if one were cut, the other would bleed –
two faces different as hot and cold.

At night, hung on the hooks on the wall
above that man's minatory head,
one wants brass where one wants gold,
one sees white and one sees black,
and one mouth eats the other
until the second sweet mouth bites back.

They dream their separate dreams
hanging on the wall above the bed.
The first voice cries: 'He's not what he seems,'
but the second one sighs: 'He is what he is,'
then one shouts 'wine' and the other screams 'bread',
and so they will all his raving days
until they die on his double-crossed head.

At signposts he must wear them both.
Each would go their separate ways
as the East or the West wind blows –
and dark and light they both would praise,
but one would melt, the other one freeze.

I am that man twice upon this time:
my two voices sing to make one rhyme.
Death I love and Death I hate,
(I'll be with you soon and late).
Love I love and Love I loathe,
God I mock and God I prove,
yes, myself I kill, myself I save.

Now, now, I hang these masks on the wall.
Oh Christ, take one and leave me all
lest four tears from two eyes fall.

The trial

The heads around the table disagree,
some say hang him from the gallows tree.

Some say high and some say low
to swing, swing, swing, when the free winds blow.

I wanted to be myself, no more,
so I screwed off the face that I always wore,

I pulled out the nails one by one –
I'd have given that face to anyone.

For those vile features were hardly mine;
to wear another's face is a spiritual crime.

Why, imagine the night when I would wed
to kiss with wrong lips in the bridal bed . . .

But now the crowd screams loud in mockery:
Oh string him up from the gallows tree.

Silence! the Judge commands, or I'll clear the court,
to hang a man up is not a sport –

though some say high and some say low
to swing, swing, swing, when the free winds blow.

Prisoner, allow me once more to ask:
what did you do with your own pure mask?

I told you, your honour, I threw it away,
it was only made of skin-coloured clay.

A face is a man, a bald juryman cries,
for one face lost, another man dies.

Gentlemen, this citizen we daren't acquit
until we know what he did with it.

It was only a face, your honour, that I lost;
how much can such a sad thing cost?

A mask is a lifetime, my bad man,
to replace such a gift nobody can.

Consider the case of that jovial swan
who took a god's face off to put a bird's face on

and Leda swooning by the side of the sea
and the swan's eyes closed in lechery.

No! No! your honour, my aim was just –
I did what every true man must.

Quiet, prisoner! Why I remember a priest remark
that he picked up a dog's face in the dark,

then he got as drunk as a man can be
and barked at God in blasphemy.

But it was a human face, sir, I cast away;
for that offence do I have to pay?

The heads around the table disagree,
some say hang him from the gallows tree.

Some say high and some say low
to swing, swing, swing, when the free winds blow.

At the back of the courtroom quietly stand
his father and mother hand-in-hand.

They can't understand the point of this case
or why he discarded his own dear face.

But it's not *my* face, father, he had said,
I don't want to die in a strange, wrong bed.

Look in the mirror, mother, stare in deep;
is that mask your own, yours to keep?

The mirror is oblong, the clock is round,
all our wax faces go underground.

Once, I built a bridge right into myself
to ransack my soul for invisible wealth

and, afterwards, I tore off my mask because
I found not the person I thought I was.

With the wrong mask, another man's life I live –
I must seek my own face, find my own grave.

The heads around the table disagree,
some say hang him from the gallows tree.

Some say high and some say low
to swing, swing, swing, when the free winds blow.

I'll sum up, the severe Judge moans,
showing the white of his knucklebones.

What is a face but the thing that you see,
the symbol and fate of identity?

How would we recognize each from each:
a dog from a man – which face on a leash?

And when tears fall where no face is,
will the tears be mine or will they be his?

To select hot coal or gold no man is free,
each choice being determined by identity.

But exchange your face then what you choose
is gained, like love, by what you lose.

Now you twelve jurymen please retire,
put your right hands in ice and your left in fire.

A hole where the face was frightens us,
and a man who can choose is dangerous.

So what is your verdict going to be,
should he be hung from a gallows tree?

Oh some say high and some say low
to swing, swing, swing, when the free winds blow.

Verses at night

Sleepless, by the windowpane I stare –
black aeroplanes displace black air.
The lazar moon glares down aghast.
The seven branched tree is bare.

Oh how much like Europe's gothic Past!
This scene my nightmare's protoplast:
glow of the radioactive worm.
Future story of the Blast?

Unreal? East and West fat Neros yearn
for other fiddled Romes to burn;
and so dogma cancels dogma
and heretics in their turn.

By my wife now, I lie quiet as a
  thought of how moon and stars might blur,
  and miles of smoke squirm overhead
    rising to Man's arbiter;

the grey skin shrivelling from the head,
  our two skulls in the double bed,
  leukaemia in the soul of all
    flowing through the blood instead.

'No,' I shout, as by her side I sprawl,
  'No,' again, as I hear my small,
  dear daughter whimper in her cot
    and across the darkness call.

New Babylons

When psaltery and dulcimer
sound the King's musick,
the plebs kneel in homage
before the Golden Image.
Shadrach, Meshach, Abed-nego,
through the open furnace go,
three only and heroic.

The Court will not adjourn.
Time's fires leap and burn
and mavericks such as I
must be branded in their turn –
to reek of human flesh
whilst venal courtiers cry:
'Conform, conform or die.'

Still I'd shout out, 'No,'
like a Daniel condemned
to prove timeless honesties.
Let spellbound lions know
an angel in the den
lest they bite to please
the vast majorities.

Outside is a lonely place.
But within, there's barely space
to embrace each other.
Edicts from the palace
as lover fumbles lover
and cynical voices cry:
'Conform, conform and die.'

Oh where is Daniel now?
Even tall rebels submit
to patterns of conformity.
I think of Babylon and admit
the hands of Time move on,
unpick us all, leave us in
uniforms of the skeleton.

Oppose, oppose, orthodoxies.
Though the furnace doors are shut,
small fires leap up high.
Cornet, drums, and sackbut,
could raise a tyrant's melodies
and the severe Judges cry:
'Conform, conform or die.'

So hearing in the Square
another maverick's despair,
as crowds draw near and shout
dark curses on the air,
where is the Daniel who
will not kneel in doubt
and will not turn about?

This, the Image of the Age:
police bring truncheons down
and each blow is our own.
When Nebuchadnezzars rage
no maverick is immune
for it's we, ourselves, who cry:
'Conform, conform and die.'

Emperors of the island

A political parable to be read aloud

There is the story of a deserted island
where five men walked down to the bay.

The story of this island is
that three men would two men slay.

Three men dug two graves in the sand,
three men stood on the sea wet rock,
three shadows moved away.

There is the story of a deserted island
where three men walked down to the bay.

The story of this island is
that two men would one man slay.

Two men dug one grave in the sand,
two men stood on the sea wet rock,
two shadows moved away.

There is the story of a deserted island
where two men walked down to the bay.

The story of this island is
that one man would one man slay.

One man dug one grave in the sand,
one man stood on the sea wet rock,
one shadow moved away.

There is the story of a deserted island
where four ghosts walked down to the bay.

The story of this island is
that four ghosts would one man slay.

Four ghosts dug one grave in the sand,
four ghosts stood on the sea wet rock;
five ghosts moved away.

Social revolution in England

Insolent as waiters, they did not ring the bell.
    Some slid down banisters, stomped up again.
    We assumed they were agencies from hell
    but why they had come no one was certain.
Best to smile like landlords, offer a jargonelle.

Number Thirteen, we said distracted, is next door.
    Often cold politeness works quite neatly.
    They brushed us aside trying to ignore
    our hints, the nice way we coughed discreetly.
They just ran up and down the staircase as before.

Preternatural bailiffs, they stripped the house bare
    of properties. Light the oblong patches
    on walls where once our gouty fathers were.
    We heard them talking in dirty snatches
as heavy doors opened. Our eyes began to blur.

It was as if we weren't, like phantoms, there at all
    and they in some intimate, cruel game
    engaged – horrid, olid, and medieval.
    Why ask why, from exactly where they came
when ergatocracies, too, in time must fall?

Who'd query such common, anonymous powers?
    By asking questions man becomes insane.
    In the empty hall now we've waited hours
    by the telephone for someone to explain,
to send some message, even if it's only flowers.

The second coming

The ground twitches and the noble head
(so often painted) breaks through the cracked crust,
hair first, then ivory forehead into the sunlit field;
the earth yields silently to the straining.
A blackbird flies away.

    The eyes open suddenly
just above the grass, seeing corn. No man is near.
Sound of days of heat, of silence.
It is lonely to be born.
And now he's breathing – air not earth
who inhaled worms and death so long.

Still his body in darkness, lightward pushing.
Pause, rest, he is tired now, enough to delight
in looking. Is this true: the world all heaven,
head in corn, with pale butterflies
staggering over him?

He cannot rise further.
The earth is heavy on his shoulders.
Cry out, shout, oh help is near.
Dangerously, the machine passes scything corn,
but the driver does not hear, cannot hear
– and now that noble head is gone,
a liquid redness in the yellow
where the mouth had been.

Dig, I say dig, you'll
find arms, loins, white legs, to prove my story –
and one red poppy in the corn.

Looking at a map

The map does not show the rain:
only pale blue for sea and Great Britain
a mosaic of multi-coloured counties
where the English weather never changes,
and the local hills and mountain ranges
are shaded heavily – though never white
as moods of snow may shade them.

Clouds never shamble over
unless this cigarette-smoke I blow out
be cloud; this sad electric bulb be sun
where constellations of flies (not planets)
all silently swing about.

False! False! Boring lines squiggle,
meaning empty roads, hedges and wet tyres;
or desolation of damp railway lines
where no one encounters a red lamp danger.
But there's menace of a kind.
Why else do official cartographers
condemn the whole land behind
a strict cage emptied of noughts and crosses
where no happy latitude is given?

And this, too, another lie:
this measurement of a lifetime's journey
in inches, these little, exact circles
for names of places where untamed people
privately hide and love and cry.

Enough, I switch off the electric bulb,
the thin current of the sun.
Oh nightly, something secret breathes and moves;
the whole flat, civilized map
that here is cracked into coloured counties,
like energy explodes, goes black;
these names of cities break out
into dotty, shifting points of glitterings,
and the light blue tide flows back.

On hearing the monologue of a deaf poet

For David Wright

People always depart, always say 'goodbye'.
You swear you can *hear* their changing faces.
I listen to careful words that falsify,
and the sincere sound of 'alas' disgraces
all purity of promises. Words die

in the air – but not on scraps of paper
that you, afflicted, could easily hoard:
snapshots of conversation fixed forever.
Ink endures, not the aural record,
not even the delirium of love's fever.

So bless the four senses that make the fifth
accept what it chooses, that may ignore
or disguise the abuse: the nameless width
of injuries, the unmitigated store
of insults, loud and authoritative.

Yet curse not the ear lightly as I do
who have the gift of hearing. I would fear
the continual sound of snow that falls on snow.
Those profound, sad silences that I hear
are enough between voices that are true.

I, like you, would rather know the shocked cries
of the animals, my child's unnecessary scream,
and praise the divine for verbal pain and lies.
Better this, than mouths moving in a dream
of the deaf where no one protests or sighs.

Though you hear very well not having heard.
And I, on this page, need write no message,
no keyless note from my clamorous world,
for doors open with the din of the image
to make audible every terrible word.

Elegy for Dylan Thomas

All down the valleys they are talking,
and in the community of the smoke-laden town.
Tomorrow, through bird-trailed skies, across labouring
waves,
wrong-again Emily will come to the dandelion yard
and, with rum tourists, inspect his grave.

Death was his voluntary marriage,
and his poor silence sold to that rich and famous bride.
Beleaguered in that essential kiss he rode
the whiskey-meadows of her breath till, mortal, voiceless,
he gave up his nailed ghost and he died.

No more to celebrate
his disinherited innocence or your half-buried heart
drunk as a butterfly, or sober as black.
Now, one second from earth, not even for the sake
of love can his true energy come back.

So cease your talking.
Too familiar you blaspheme his name and collected legends:
some tears fall soundlessly and aren't the same
as those that drop with obituary explosions.
Suddenly, others who sing seem older and lame.

But far from the blind country of prose,
wherever his burst voice goes about you or through you,
look up in surprise, in a hurt public house
or in a rain-blown street, and see how
no fat ghost but a quotation cries.

Stranger, he is laid to rest
not in the nightingale dark nor in the canary light.
At the dear last, the yolk broke in his head,
blood of his soul's egg in a splash of bright
voices and now he is dead.

December, 1953

Go home the act is over

Roll up, roll up, the circus has begun,
a Dionysian poet will perform.
Listen, two dwarfs beat thunder on a drum
and whizzing spotlights flash as in a storm.

Look, like a trapeze artist, he flies with wires
above spectators who with iambics freeze.
To those with cold hands he offers fires
and sings the catastrophes.

Blow gaudy trumpets then, let the lions roar,
the circus crowd is ready. You others,
is it his death you're waiting for?
Where any poet sings the vulture hovers.

Electrician on the balcony, point the light.
Tall against the roof his two shadows dance
and somersault. He sings for your delight,
but seeing gold, trips and loses balance.

The audience is hushed. The sawdust ring
is empty except where that singer lies.
Still, high in the air, two trapezes swing.
Does that last image leak from his two eyes?

Return now to that place. The grass instead,
the wind and stars where once the spotlights shone.
His funambulists and jugglers are dead.
The show is over. The big tent gone.

Enter The Movement

They said proudly, 'Our demon', pointing to
the Boat-house and the famous tenant who
sang in the night with half the lights put out.
Sometimes his song was true, no mere ranting shout.

Sensual intruders rejoiced and danced
to his gorgeous music and, if in time, it chanced
the ceiling sagged with sound and the walls cracked,
well, he sang the Welsh passion others lacked.

His powerful voice broke all the windows,
which transparencies must be paid in prose
not by wild fictions of a singing clown.
Some applauded when his roof fell down.

Then winter came when whistling beggars freeze.
He, to quench inner fires, drank catastrophes
while corybants, roaring, jigged with joy outside
till, delirious, that lyric singer died.

Now all cry, 'Regard that desperate ruin
of a life, example of Dionysian sin,'
and begin to rebuild, replace the roof,
finding one devil damnable enough.

The new choir that moves in is neat and sane
and dare not whistle in the dark again.
Proudly English, they sing with sharp, flat voices
but no-one dances, nobody rejoices.

The moment

You raise your eyes from the level book
as if deeply listening. You are further than I call.
Like Eurydice you wear a hurt and absent look,
but I'm gentle for the silence into which you fall so
sadly.
What are you thinking? Do you love me?
Suddenly you are not you at all but a ghost
dreaming of a castle to haunt or a heavy garden;
some place eerie, and far from me. But now a door
is banging outside, so you turn your head surprised.

You speak my name and someone else has died.

Poem and message

Out on the tormented, midnight sea
your sails are blown in jeopardy.
Gales of grief and terrors force
you from the spirit's chartered course.

But, in the storm, lighthouses mark
rocks of dangers in the dark;
so from this shore of cold I write
tiny flashes in the night.

Words of safety, words of love,
a beacon in the dark to save
you from the catastrophic sea,
and navigate you home to me.

Dear, vague as a distant star, I,
in the huge night's amorphous lie,
find one small and luminous truth
of which our usual love was proof.

And I call your name as loud I can
and give you all the light I am.

Anniversary

The tree grows down from a bird.
The strong grass pulls up the earth
to a hill. Wade here, my dear,
through green shallows of daisies.
I hear the voice talking that is dead
behind the voice that is talking now.
The clocks of the smoky town
strike a quiet, grating sound.
Tomorrow will be the same.
Two sit on this hill and count
two moving from the two that stayed.

What happens to a flame blown out?
What perishes? Not this view,
nor my magnified hand in yours
whatever hurt and angers done.
I breathe in air the dead breathed out.
When first you inclined your face
to mine, my sweet ally came,
with your brown eyes purely wide.
My right hand on your left breast
I said, I have little to tell my dear.
For the pure bird, a pure cage.

Oh the silence that you lost
blind in the pandemonium
of the kiss and ruined was.
My dear, my dear, what perishes?
I hear this voice in a voice to come.

Poem of celebration

I lean against the air.
It gives way like unstitched water. I fall in
but am drowned in air. Now distinctly
every image reflects the invisible world.

The noise divides from the light.
Bold astronomers who at night
peep through the window-pane of the colossal skies
look too far for the furthest star.
This world confirms my senses.

Swaying and drunk with seeing
the near magnificence of things,
I cry out a doxology with the surprise
of a shout, creating maximum silence.

How else may I give thanks, give praise,
but to trap a visible poem
in the invisible cage and leave it there?
Look, I'm back again to where you are.
I came through a hole in the air.

Enriched forever. Hardly evangelical
but still my rainbowed heart blessed and thumping.
Any man may gather the images of despair;
I'll say 'I will' and 'I can'
and like an accident breathe in space and air.

The Victim of Aulis

A multitude of masts in the harbour.
The sails limp in the air, becalmed.
The tired sea barely moving.
    The sea breathes quietly, Agamemnon.
        The wind is dead.
The sunlight leaping the waters,
the waters lapping at the boats.
Heat haze.
The King prowls the still deck
back and fore while the Captains quarrel.
We only throw dice and curse.
    The child! The child!
The whisper of the sea, the secret of the sea;
the sea is dreaming and a tall slave sings.
    What are we to do?
        They will think of a way.
            We have had nothing of education.
                We must obey, being little men.
                    The cause is just.
                        Leave it to the Captains.
                            What does Calchas say?
                                The child! The child!
And we thinking of our own daughters
with clumsy father-pride,
though those other virgins are faceless now
indistinct as the mingling of voices,
as the shuffle of the sea,
the little sound of the sea.
    It has been a long time.
        Leave it to the priests.
Conference at Aulis.

And he, the King, listening to the whisper of Calchas,
to the sea restless in its sleep while a tall slave sings –
sings of home and alien distances,
a slow voice, sad as a light,
as a flame burning in daytime.
  Agamemnon is in religion.
    It's that or nothing now.
      The child! The child!
And she peering down through the fathomless minds
of the sea, at green shadows and dark dreams of fish –
for the deep thoughts of the sea are fish –
and she trailing her small hands in the waters
playing with coloured beads of spray.
  Come with me.
    Why father?
We sit on the stone quay with the sun and the seagulls.
  We know nothing of rough mythologies, only
      fact.
    We need the gods more than they need us.
      And never will some come home again.
Artemis is offended, Calchas said,
staring at golden bangles spinning on the sea,
at arrows of poisoned sunlight pricking the flat sea;
the yellow masts vertical, pointing at the blue, luxurious sky,
the white sails lagging down, without life, without wind.
Calchas mumbles: Troy, Troy.
We only throw dice and curse the dawn we sailed away,
grumble and tell lewd tales of faithless women,
remembering Helen ravished in a foreign bed.
  The child! The child!
And the King musing: what will her mother say?

The sigh and the sadness of it. And she who has no breasts
trailing her small hands in the waters, just a child,
still a child – that is a fearful thing.
   Come with me.
      Why father?
Murder at Aulis.
Oh the questions of the young-to-be-slain,
and the memory of black eyelashes pulled apart suddenly
revealing more white of the eye than a man bargained for.
The King is in religion
whose name is great among the Greeks –
the blood, ridiculously crimson in the groves of Artemis,
and the wind howling, why father? why father?
for many days and louder in the silence of the night,
and dispossessed and possessing him in the mornings,
in the sea-spray climbing, and in the sea-howl,
as the fleet drags on aslant in the furious wind.
They thought of a way.
We are little men
who follow and obey
as the cracked sails billow out half below the leaping sea,
as the tall slave sings why Father? why Father?

The game

Follow the crowds to where the turnstiles click.
The terraces fill. *Hoompa*, blares the brassy band.
Saturday afternoon has come to Ninian Park
and, beyond the goal posts, in the Canton Stand
between black spaces, a hundred matches spark.

Waiting, we recall records, legendary scores:
Fred Keenor, Hardy, in a royal blue shirt.
The very names, sad as the old songs, open doors
before our time where someone else was hurt.
Now, like an injured beast, the great crowd roars.

The coin is spun. Here all is simplified,
and we are partisan who cheer the Good,
hiss at passing Evil. Was Lucifer offside?
A wing falls down when cherubs howl for blood.
Demons have agents: the Referee is bribed.

The white ball smacked the crossbar. Satan rose
higher than the others in the smoked brown gloom
to sink on grass in a ballet dancer's pose.
Again, it seems, we hear a familiar tune
not quite identifiable. A distant whistle blows.

Memory of faded games, the discarded years;
talk of Aston Villa, Orient, and the Swans.
Half-time, the band played the same military airs
as when the Bluebirds once were champions.
Round touchlines the same cripples in their chairs.

Mephistopheles had his joke. The honest team
dribbles ineffectively, no one can be blamed.
Infernal backs tackle, inside forwards scheme,
and if they foul us need we be ashamed?
Heads up! Oh for a Ted Drake, a Dixie Dean.

'Saved' or else, discontents, we are transferred
long decades back, like Faust must pay that fee.
The night is early. Great phantoms in us stir
as coloured jerseys hover, move diagonally
on the damp turf, and our eidetic visions blur.

God sign our souls! Because the obscure staff
of Hell rule this world, jugular fans guessed
the result halfway through the second half,
and those who know the score just seem depressed.
Small boys swarm the field for an autograph.

Silent the stadium. The crowds have all filed out.
Only the pigeons beneath the roofs remain.
The clean programmes are trampled underfoot,
and natural the dark, appropriate the rain,
whilst, under lamp-posts, threatening newsboys
  shout.

The race

We three crouched down ready to go,
Past, Present and Future. Although
the race was rigged, we didn't know.

Now, my head low in shy disgrace,
I move into the second place
and try to hold this killing pace

and gain my second breath. I curse,
seeing the countryside in reverse:
the road slide back to where I was.

I feel my formed face change. And run
yet faster to let Thy Will be done.
Look, I spurt towards Kingdom Come.

Behind me I hear the Present shout:
'Why don't they jeer and carry me out;
what is the silence all about?'

The old dream I carry on my back
is the chaos the other two lack.
I sprint to the inside of the track.

Drawing near I hear the Future cry,
'I am your death and prophecy,
but in transforming you I die.'

Just in front that champion lies.
Our four legs together harmonize
till I pass him for the final prize.

In the stadium the brash crowd roar.
I know what they are calling for;
but will my fading dream endure?

Here is the Hangman and the Tree,
shapes of some green allegory;
I run towards the world to be.

Now I'm the Future who was the Past,
at last I lead who once was last.
I round another lap, sprinting fast.

Ahead I see the winning post.
I finish first and so have lost
and speed into my walking ghost.

Public library

Who, in the public library, one evening after rain,
amongst the polished tables and linoleum,
stands bored under blank light to glance at these
 pages?
Whose absent mood, like neon glowing in the night,
is conversant with wet pavements, nothing to do?

Neutral, the clock-watching girl stamps out the date,
a forced celebration, a posthumous birthday,
her head buttered by the drizzling library lamps;
yet the accident of words, too, can light the
semi-dark
should the reader lead them home, generously
journey,
later to return, perhaps leaving a bus ticket as a
bookmark.

Who wrote in margins hieroglyphic notations,
that obscenity, deleted this imperfect line?
Read by whose hostile eyes, in what bed-sitting
rooms,
in which rainy, dejected railway stations?

The water diviner

Late, I have come to a parched land
doubting my gift, if gift I have,
the inspiration of water
spilt, swallowed in the sand.

To hear once more water trickle,
to stand in a stretch of silence
the divine pen twisting in the hand:
sign of depths alluvial.

Water owns no permanent shape,
brags, is most itself in chaos;
now, under the shadow of the idol,
dry mouth and dry landscape.

No rain falls with a refreshing sound
to settle tubular in a well,
elliptical in a bowl. No grape
lusciously moulds it round.

Clouds have no constant resemblance
to anything, blown by a hot wind,
flying mirages; the blue background,
light constructions of chance.

To hold back chaos I transformed
amorphous mass: clay, fire, or cloud,
so that the agèd gods might dance
and golden structures form.

I should have built, plain brick on brick,
a water tower. The sun flies on
arid wastes, barren hells too warm
and me with a hazel stick!

Rivulets vanished in the dust
long ago, great compositions
vaporized, salt on the tongue so thick
that drinking, still I thirst.

Repeated desert, recurring drought,
sometimes hearing water trickle,
sometimes not, I, by doubting first,
believe; believing, doubt.

Return to Cardiff

'Hometown'; well, most admit an affection for a city:
grey, tangled streets I cycled on to school, my first cigarette
in the back lane, and, fool, my first botched love affair.
First everything. Faded torments; self-indulgent pity.

The journey to Cardiff seemed less a return than a raid
on mislaid identities. Of course the whole locus smaller:
the mile-wide Taff now a stream, the castle not as in some
black,
gothic dream, but a decent sprawl, a joker's toy façade.

Unfocused voices in the wind, associations, clues,
odds and ends, fringes caught, as when, after the doctor quit,
a door opened and I glimpsed the white, enormous face
of my grandfather, suddenly aghast with certain news.

Unable to define anything I can hardly speak,
and still I love the place for what I wanted it to be
as much as for what it unashamedly is
now for me, a city of strangers, alien and bleak.

Unable to communicate I'm easily betrayed,
uneasily diverted by mere sense reflections
like those anchored waterscapes that wander, alter, in the
Taff,
hour by hour, as light slants down a different shade.

Illusory, too, that lost dark playground after rain,
the noise of trams, gunshots in what they once called Tiger
Bay.
Only real this smell of ripe, damp earth when the sun comes
out,
a mixture of pungencies, half exquisite and half plain.

No sooner than I'd arrived the other Cardiff had gone,
smoke in the memory, these but tinned resemblances,
where the boy I was not and the man I am not
met, hesitated, left double footsteps, then walked on.

Chalk

Chalk, calcium carbonate, should mean school –
a small, neutral stick neither cool nor hot,
its smell should evoke wooden desks slamming
when, squeaking over blackboards, it could not
decently teach us more than one plus one.

Now, no less pedagogic in ruder districts,
on iron railway bridges, where urchins fight,
an urgent scrawl names our failure – BAN THE BOMB,
or more peculiarly, KEEP BRITAIN WHITE.
Chalk, it seems, has some bleeding purposes.

In the night, secretly, they must have come,
strict, clenched men in the street, anonymous,
past closed shops and the sound of running feet
till upstairs, next morning, vacant in a bus,
we observe a once blank wall assaulted.

There's not enough chalk in the wronged world
to spell out one plus one, the perfect lies.
HANDS OFF GUATEMALA – though slogans change,
never the chalk scraping on the pitched noise
of a nerve in violence or in longing.

Summer's Sunday song

At this village, religious as a psalm,
  peaceful by this English river's edge,
light visits the undersides of bridges,
  midges dare the olive waters calm.
    Come prepare yourself, disarm.

Where punt, and willow tree, and swan contend
for mastery of the humbled eye,
even Ophelia could come floating by
consoled. Inaudible organs sound.
Now advance on lyric ground.

Late, the sun clings on biscuit-coloured walls
of mellowed farmhouse, hallowed chapel.
Smoked gold shafts ignite high branches, dapple
the woods with shadows. This path compels.
Green vibrating fields like bells.

Grave nature, how the pious dark is pale,
trippers in the gloom restart their cars.
Let the ear (thatched roofs sag below the stars)
usurp the eye: owl and nightingale
orchestrate your holy tale.

Sunday evening

Loved not for themselves those tenors who sing
arias from 'Aïda' on horned, tinny
gramophones – but because they take a man back
to a half forgotten thing.

We, transported by this evening loaded
with a song recorded by Caruso,
recall some other place, another time,
now charmingly outmoded.

What, for wrong motives, too often is approved
proves we once existed, becomes mere flattery
– then it's ourselves whom we are listening to,
and, by hearing, we are moved.

To know, haunted, this echo too will fade
with fresh alliteration of the leaves,
as more rain, indistinct, drags down the sky
like a sense of gloom mislaid.

Dear classic, melodic absences
how stringently debarred, kept out of mind,
till some genius on a gramophone
holes defences, breaks all fences.

What lives in a man and calls him back
and back through desolate Sunday evenings?
Indescribable, oh faint generic name:
sweet taste, bitter lack.

The magician

Off stage, the Great Illusionist owns bad teeth,
cheats at cards, beats his second wife, is lewd;
before studying his art he qualified
as obsessional liar, petty thief.

Transformed by glamorous paraphernalia –
tall top hat, made-up face, four smoking spotlights –
only fellow magicians can sense beneath
that glossy surface, a human failure.

Ready with unseen wires, luminous paint,
with drums and ceremony he fills the stage,
rich twice nightly in his full regalia.
Two extras planted in the audience faint.

Allezup! Closes his eyes, seemingly bored,
and astutely fakes a vulgar miracle,
mutters and reclines to become fakir, saint;
on a hotbed of nails, swallows a sword.

For encore will saw a seedy blonde in half
as music rises to a shrill crescendo;
hacks through wood, skin, vertebrae, spinal cord,
and all except the gods applaud or laugh.

Lord, red blood oozes from the long black box,
oh hocus pocus, oh abracadabra,
whilst, in trumped-up panic, manager and staff
race breathlessly on stage, undo the locks.

Patrons prefer bisected blondes to disappear.
Relieved, commercial men and their average wives
now salaciously prepare for further shocks,
eagerly yearn to see what they most fear.

Sometimes, something he cannot understand
happens – atavistic powers stray unleashed,
a raving voice he hardly thought to hear,
the ventriloquist's dummy out of hand.

In the box, a vision of himself – and on
those masochistic nails fresh genuine blood,
within his white glove a decomposing hand,
and, unimaginably, his own face gone.

Quite disturbed the disconnected audience boo.
What cheek! This charlatan believes his magic:
not luminous paint across the darkness shone
when, happily, for once, his lies came true.

Or so it seemed. Oh what overbearing pride
if no longer fake but Great Illusionist;
but as phony critics pierce him through and through
he begs for mercy and is justified.

Off stage, that Great Illusionist owns bad teeth,
cheats at cards, beats his second wife, is lewd;
before studying his art he qualified
as obsessional liar, petty thief.

The French master

Everyone in Class II at the Grammar School
had heard of Walter Bird, known as Wazo.
They said he'd behead each dullard and fool
or, instead, carve off a tail for the fun.

Wazo's cane buzzed like a bee in the air.
Quietly, quietly, in the desks of Form III
sneaky Wazo tweaked our ears and our hair.
Walter Wazo, public enemy No. 1.

Five feet tall, he married sweet Doreen Wall,
and combmarks furrowed his vaselined hair;
his hands still fluttered ridiculously small,
his eyes the colour of a poison bottle.

Who'd think he'd falter, poor love-sick Walter
as bored he read out *Lettres de mon Moulin*;
his mouth had begun to soften and alter,
and Class IV ribbed him as only boys can.

Perhaps through kissing his wife to a moan
had alone changed the shape of his lips,
till the habit of her mouth became his own:
no more Walter Wazo, enemy No. 1.

'Boy', he'd whine, 'yes, please decline the verb to
  have,'
in tones dulcet and mild as a girl.
'Sorry sir, can't sir, must go to the lav,'
whilst Wazo stared out of this world.

Till one day in May Wazo buzzed like a bee
and stung, twice, many a warm, inky hand;
he stormed through the form, a catastrophe,
returned to this world, No. 1.

Alas, alas, to the Vth Form's disgrace
nobody could quote Villon to that villain.
Again the nasty old mouth zipped on his face,
and not a weak-bladdered boy in the class.

Was Doreen being kissed by a Mr Anon?
Years later, I purred, 'Your dear wife, Mr Bird?'
Teeth bared, how he *glared* before stamping on;
and suddenly I felt sorry for the bastard.

At the Tate

If the dead owned ears that refused to crumble
perhaps they would hear one sound forever
from yesterday or patient years ago:
either the bellowing in the crematorium
or the earth rumbling down on the coffin.
'La vie, cette merveille,' cried Rodin, but the dead
accuse Creation, resemble stone.
This dolorous thought first, then the sculpture,
the embodiment of an illusion.
Shoes squeaking, autumn sunlight, parquet floors,
as Rodin's lovers keep on kissing

and not kissing. These statues are listening
not to their own heartbeats, erotic sighs,
immoderate, endearing promises,
nor to knowing voices: 'How Rodin praised Life!'
Rather they hear, if they hear at all,
always and haunted, between intervals
of a silence that is not the silence here,
one man's exhalations of discontent –
the sculptor muttering, 'Toujours travailler,'
and, blow after blow, the noise of hammer
on chisel, the protracted cry of surfaces.
Most statues seem sad and introspective,
they hold their breath between coming and going,
they lament their devoured, once shuddering stone.

The shunters

The colour of grief, and thoroughly tame,
the shunters slave on silver parallels.
Propitious their proletarian numbers.
Only posh expresses sport proper names.

In the tired afternoon drizzle, their smoke
fades into industrial England.
Governed by levers, hearing clanking chains,
how can a smudge of engines run amok?

Rain drags darkness down where shunters work
the blank gloom below hoardings, dejected sheds,
below yellow squares in backs of tenements
whilst, resigned, charcoal trucks clash and jerk.

A prince is due. Like victims shunters wait
meekly – *The Red Dragon? The Devon Belle?*
A crash of lights. Four o'clock schoolboys gape
over the bridge, inarticulate.

Later, late, again, far their echoes rage;
hurt, plaintive whistles; hyphenated trucks;
sexual cries from funnels – all punctuate
the night, a despair beyond language.

Tree

Grotesquely shaped, this stubbed tree craves a madman's
  eye,
its convoluted pipes lie tortured on the air,
twist black, turn back to fanged twigs and attitudes,
its dusty leaves quite stunted, still it will not die.

In rousing spring its frugal green was last to bud,
in autumn will be the first to anticipate the fall.
Now, aimlessly, I give it human attributes:
its mud-coloured bark, sick flesh; sap, a victim's blood.

As, sometimes, a child, contorting his plastic face
to make another laugh, is told to cease his play
lest abstract fate solidifies both lips and eyes,
horrifically, to one perpetual grimace;

so, perhaps, this maimed structure postured once and thus –
a buffoon amidst these oaks. Then laughter shook
untimely leaves down till avenging lightning struck,
petrified the attitude, a spectacle for us.

August – other trees conform, are properly dressed;
but this funny one exists for funny children,
easy to climb, easy to insult, or throw stones at,
and only urgent lovers in its shade will rest.

Yet this pauper, this caliban tree, let good men praise,
for it survives, and that's enough; more, on gala nights,
with copper beech and silver birch it too can soar
unanchored, free, in prosperous moonlight and amaze.

Odd

In front of our house in Golders Green
the lawn, like a cliché, mutters, 'Rose bushes.'
The whole suburb is very respectable.
Ugly men drive past in funeral suits,
from their necks you can tell they're overweight.

Sodium lamp-posts, at night, hose empty roads
with gold which treacles over pavement trees,
polishes brittle hedges, clings on closed, parked cars.
If a light should fly on in an upstairs room
odds on two someones are going to sleep.

It's unusual to meet a beggar,
you hardly ever see a someone drunk.
It's a nice, clean, quiet, religious place.
For my part, now and then, I want to scream:
thus, by the neighbours, am considered odd.

From the sensible wastes of Golders Green
I journey to Soho where a job owns me.
Soho is not a respectable place.
Underweight women in the gamiest of skirts
bleed a smile of false teeth at ugly men.

Later, the dark is shabby with paste electric
of peeporamas, brothels, clubs and pubs,
restaurants that sport sallow waiters who cough.
If a light should fly on in an upstairs room
odds on two someones are going to bed.

It's customary to see many beggars,
common to meet people roaring and drunk.
It's a nice, loud, dirty, irreligious place.
For my part, now and then, I want to scream:
thus, by Soho friends, am considered odd.

After the release of Ezra Pound

In Jerusalem I asked
the ancient Hebrew poets to forgive you,
and what would Walt Whitman have said
and Thomas Jefferson? [*Paul Potts*]

In Soho's square mile of unoriginal sin
where the fraudulent neon lights haunt,
but cannot hide, the dinginess of vice,
the jeans and sweater boys spoke of Pound,
and you, Paul, repeated your question.

The chi-chi bums in Torino's laughed and
the virgins of St Martin's School of Art.
The corner spivs with their Maltese masks
loitered for the two o'clock result,
and those in the restaurants of Greek Street,
eating income tax, did not hear the laugh.

Gentle Gentile, you asked the question.
Free now (and we praise this) Pound could answer.

The strip lighting of Soho did not fuse,
no blood trickled from a certain book
down the immaculate shelves of Zwemmer's.
But the circumcised did not laugh.
The swart nudes in the backrooms put on clothes
and the doors of the French pub closed.

Pound did not hear the raw Jewish cry,
the populations committed to the dark
when he muttered through microphones
of murderers. He, not I, must answer.

Because of the structures of a beautiful poet
you ask the man who is less than beautiful,
and wait in the public neurosis of Soho,
in the liberty of loneliness for an answer.

In the beer and espresso bars they talked
of Ezra Pound, excusing the silences of an old man,
saying there is so little time between
the parquet floors of an institution
and the boredom of the final box.

Why, Paul, if that ticking distance between
was merely a journey long enough
to walk the circumference of a Belsen,
Walt Whitman would have been eloquent,
and Thomas Jefferson would have cursed.

Spring, 1958

Red balloon

It sailed across the startled town,
over chapels, over chimney-pots,
wind-blown above a block of flats
before it floated down.

Oddly, it landed where I stood,
and finding's keeping, as you know.
I breathed on it, I polished it,
till it shone like living blood.

It was my shame, it was my joy,
it brought me notoriety.
From all of Wales the rude boys came,
it ceased to be a toy.

I heard the girls of Cardiff sigh
when my balloon, my red balloon,
soared higher like a happiness
towards the dark blue sky.

Nine months since, have I boasted of
my unique, my only precious;
but to no one dare I show it now
however long they swear their love.

'It's a Jew's balloon,' my best friend cried,
'stained with our dear Lord's blood.'
'That I'm a Jew is true,' I said,
said I, 'that cannot be denied.'

'What relevance?' I asked, surprised,
'what's religion to do with this?'
'Your red balloon's a Jew's balloon,
let's get it circumcised.'

Then some boys laughed and some boys cursed,
some unsheathed their dirty knives;
some lunged, some clawed at my balloon,
but still it would not burst.

They bled my nose, they cut my eye,
half conscious in the street I heard,
'Give up, give up your red balloon.'
I don't know exactly why.

Father, bolt the door, turn the key,
lest those sad, brash boys return
to insult my faith and steal
my red balloon from me.

Postmark

Envelopes that come with an official stamp,
to conjure up visions of IN and OUT trays,
make me think of death, of Jewish funerals,
lost afternoons faded and damp.

Of course it's a private association.
Other happenings may signify – maybe
a picture frame that falls down, suddenly, prompts
you to morbid speculation.

Anyway, the dead were alien as could be,
fit for red tape, odd names on a *proforma*;
even their relatives gathering had little,
if anything, to do with me.

Till one laundry-coloured, sky-blown day,
  a telegram –
then a phone clamouring in a quiet hall
immured a familiar though stylized voice:
synagogue doors began to slam.

Pecking typewriters were hushed, an unseen staff
filed in and out subdued, put slang in a drawer,
as I whispered above the wail of Yiddish
so shocked that I wanted to laugh.

Yet I inhabited a serious suit;
black tie, armband; an uncreased face to match;
observed dust in sunbeams whilst knowing uncles
washed dry hands, appeared astute,

owned an awkward correctness as can be found
in civic buildings (whose linoleum smell
wafts along corridors to offices where,
on Sundays, there is not a sound).

Though a mere youth I'd heard about this pogrom
or that – and thought, whether in York or in Dachau,
Death had something to do with the Government.
Nobody told me I was wrong.

I don't know why else an official postmark
should make me think thus. He whom I mourned is
half forgot: a sandpaper chin, a smile, a voice,
and the rest is not silence but dark.

The grand view

Mystics, in their far, erotic stance,
neglect our vulgar catastrophes.
I, with cadence, rhyme and assonance,
must pardon their oceanic trance,
their too saintlike immoralities.

For I, too, spellbound by the grand view,
flung through vistas from this windy hill,
am in pure love. I do not know who
it is that I love, but I would flow
into One invisible and still.

Though islanded and inspired by
the merely human, I sing back robes of air
to uncover my ego-plundered eye,
abandoning my apostasy,
no more to make a home out of despair.

Only Moses on the high mountain
at least knew what he was climbing for.
God-haunted, wonderstruck, half insane,
that condemned genius brought down again
ten social poems we call the law.

My littleness makes but a private sound,
the little lyric of a little man;
yet, like Moses, I walk on holy ground
since all earth is, and the world is round
I come back to where he began.

My forehead is open. The horns grow out
and exit. Infirm cynics knock inside,
and still ancestral voices shout
visions, visions! Should I turn about
if, by naming all, One is denied?

There are moments when a man must sing
of a lone Presence he cannot see.
To undulations of space I bring
all my love when love is happening;
green directions flying back to me.

There are moments when a man must praise
the astonishment of being alive,
when small mirrors of reality blaze
into miracles; and there's One always
who, by never departing, almost arrives.

Sunsets

1

This scene too beautiful it seems a fake,
these unlikely colours, this sky, that lake.
I have to close my eyes to keep awake.

Were all such lucid colours moving greys,
God's formal barbarities would amaze.
There is nothing else I may do but praise.

But speaking, I move into a future tense
to gain mere words, and lose the quiet sense
of wonder, destroying the experience.

Sunsets only exist that I may write
about them; yet I'd dip my pen in light:
white print obscurely on a page of white.

2

Darkness, like terror, lies within the scene.
Music of Mozart merely seems serene.
He gazed at green till he became the green.

Mystics to keep awake close their eyes,
and, in eternal emptiness, feel wise.
God is what that great nothing signifies.

Oh the beautiful eyes of St Lucy
who plucked them out that she might see.
Such was her devotion to the Mystery.

The distance between two stars is night.
I stare and stare at dark till dark is bright.
Must I first go blind to have second sight?

3

Above that painted lake (of course unsigned)
its surface hoofed by colours in the wind,
there were windows between clouds and fires behind.

Light that irradiates is never dead,
so that violent heaven now lies in the head
and agonies of sky grow dark instead.

Past midnight, I re-create the gorgeous air
of sunset, its adorations of despair.
I stared at colour till I was the stare.

But since I can't breathe always with the five
senses naked, I wait for sleep to arrive,
and close both my eyes to keep alive.

Surprise! Surprise!

Talk not of loneliness, but aloneness.
Every thing is alien, everyone strange.
Regard an object closely, our own foot
named, how queer it appears as its toes flex.

Peer at it with greenhorn observation;
thus magnified, what incongruous toenails!
Or the tree outside, we pass every day,
stand below it, stare at it flagrantly
till it becomes uncomfortable, till
its slender boughs, shyly naked beneath
those veined, pellucid leaves, stir a little.
Scrutinized, it grows unrecognizable.
Again, utterly estranged, our colleague
who talks to us on weekdays – just the way
he walks, what a peculiar, indolent
manner of walking, come to think of it;
and lastly, that woman we love fondly,
sounded and labelled, who loves us perhaps,
look how she, while reading the newspaper,
taps her own forehead, checks her cheek, cheekbone,
nose, her martial lip, over and over,
withdrawn in concentration, unaware,
yet feels her face to affirm it's still there.
How then can we whisper, at night, 'My own'?
Oh how everything and everybody
are perplexed and perplexing, deeply unknown.
What surprises is that sometimes we are
not surprised, that a door clicks, half opens,
and we guessed beforehand who would enter.
Is that why we dare to cry: 'I know Smith'?
Now, which of you, suggesting I raise my head
from this page, will call my name familiarly?
You will see, as always, my eyes startled.

Two voices

I *A woman to a man*

To own nothing, but to be –
like the vagrant wind that bears
faintest fragrance of the sea
or, in anger, lifts and tears
yet hoards no property;

I praise that state of mind:
wind, music, and you, are such.
All the visible you find
(the invisible you touch)
alter, and leave behind.

To pure being you devote
all your days. You are your eyes,
seemingly near but remote.
Gone, now, the sense of surprise,
like a dying musical note.

Like fragrance, you left no trace,
like anger, you came my way,
like music, you filled the space
(by going, the more you stay).
Departures were in your face.

2 *A wife to a husband*

Doth the music always flee?
Who kiss, that they may own,
sing happily, oh happily
of brick on brick till stone
keeps out both wind and sea.

So come back fast, come back slow,
I'll be distance and your home,
every symbol that I know,
church, tower, mosque, and dome,
then by staying, the more you'll go.

Let me breathe in music where
I am nothing but your life;
your designs, directions share,
to be no mistress but a wife,
pluck your meanings from the air.

I'll be all things you would be,
the four winds and the seven seas,
you'll play with such a gaiety
devastating melodies
till music be my body.

After a departure

Intimate god of stations,
on long, faded afternoons
before impatient trains depart,
where the aching lovers wait
and mothers embarrass sons,
discover your natural art;
delicately articulate
an elegy of the heart
for horizons appropriate,
or dialogues for the stage
and the opening of an eye.

Love invents the sadness of
tolerable departures.
So bless every fumbling kiss
when eyes, hands, lips, betray
shy, tentative disclosures,
conclusions that non-lovers miss.
Taxis, buses, surge away
through the grey metropolis
while mortals frown for words to say,
and their ordinary messages
approximate, therefore lie.

Those heroes who departed
spouting famous monologues
were more verbose than we.
Antony at Paddington,
bizarre in his Roman togs,
a sword clanking on his knee,
would have jabbered on and on

love epithets most happily,
well after the train had gone.
Let prosy travellers rage
long as Cleopatras sigh.

Romeo's peroration
for Juliet at Waterloo,
as gulps of steam arise
from the engine on its bit,
and from station-masters too,
would bring tears to the eyes.
Sooty god of stations permit
your express to dally, revise
timetables, dull schedules if it
allows one more classic page
or a Juliet to cry.

Today, I, your professional
pleb of words who must appear
spontaneous, who knows form
to be decorative logic,
whose style is in the error,
ask forgiveness for my storm
of silence when all speech grew sick;
who, waving from the platform,
found even gesture ironic,
afraid of your beautiful coinage
'I love you' and 'Goodbye'.

From a suburban window

Such afternoon glooms, such clouds chimney low –
London, the clouds want to move but can not,
London, the clouds want to rain but can not –
such negatives of a featureless day:
the street empty but for a van passing,
an afternoon smudged by old afternoons.
Soon, despite railings, evening will come
from a great distance trailing evenings.
Meantime, unemployed sadness loiters here.

Quite suddenly, six mourners appear:
a couple together, then three stout men,
then one more, lagging behind, bare-headed.
Not one of the six looks up at the sky,
and not one of them touches the railings.
They walk on and on remembering days,
yet seem content. They employ the décor.
They use this grey inch of eternity,
and the afternoon, so praised, grows distinct.

Close up

Often you seem to be listening to a music
that others cannot hear. Rilke would have loved you:
you never intrude, you never ask questions
of those, crying in the dark, who are most near.

You always keep something of yourself to yourself
in the electric bars, even in bedrooms.
Rilke would have praised you: your nearness is far,
and, therefore, your distance like the very stars.

Yet some things you miss and some things you lose
by keeping your arm outstretched; and some things
you'll never know unless one, at least, knows you
like a close-up, in detail – blow by human blow.

As I was saying

Yes, madam, as a poet I *do* take myself seriously,
and, since I have a young, questioning family, I suppose
I should know something about English wild flowers:
the shape of their leaves, when this and that one grows,
how old mythologies attribute strange powers
to this or that one. Urban, I should mug up anew
the pleasant names: Butterbur, Ling, and Lady's Smock,
Jack-by-the-Hedge, Cuckoo-Pint, and Feverfew,
even the Stinking Hellebore – all in that W. H. Smith book
I could bring home for myself (inscribed to my daughter)
to swot, to know which is this and which that one,
what honours the high cornfield, what the low water,
under the slow-pacing clouds and occasional sun of England.
    But no! Done for in the ignorant suburb,
I'll drink Scotch, neurotically stare through glass
at the rainy lawn, at green stuff, nameless birds,

and let my daughter, madam, go to nature class.
I'll not compete with those nature poets you advance,
some in country dialect, and some in dialogue
with the country – few as calm as their words:
Wordsworth, Barnes, sad John Clare who ate grass.

Olfactory pursuits

Often, unobserved, I smell my own hand.
I am searching for something forgotten.
I bang the door behind me, breathing in.

I think that a bitter or candied scent
is like a signpost pointing backwards
on which is writ no place and no distance.

So I walk towards a Verulamium,
your ruins or my ruins. The sun's ambushed:
fleeing on the ground the same, large shadow.

Look up. There's no smell to the colour blue.
The wind blew it right through the spaces
between clouds. Christ, what is it I'm after?

I dream, without sleeping, of things obscure,
of houses and streets and temples deserted
which, if once visited, I don't recall.

Here are a few stones instead of a wall,
and here broken stones instead of a house.
Hopelessly, with odours I conjoin.

My footfall echoes down old foundations,
buried mosaics, tomb tablets crumbled,
flints in the grass, your ruins or my ruins.

A man sniffs the back of his own hand,
moistens it with his mouth, to sniff again,
to think a blank; writes, 'The odour of stones.'

Halls

Halls of houses own a sweet biscuity smell;
and the carpet's frayed, the staircase lonely.

The landing light belongs to winter evenings.
When empty, all doors closed, the hall's itself.

It becomes an ear. Aware of a loud party
behind walls, and of cartilage clicking in a knee.

Between the porch and the head's eyes in a living room
it is the eight paces that can alter a man.

No wonder our grandfathers put clocks in halls,
and percussed barometers hopefully.

Lest the hall betray the host's formidable smile,
guests ushered in are not enticed to linger.

Later, guests leaving, slightly drunk, deranged,
neither know the hall nor the host, smileless.

What's detained by loitering, in gloomy halls,
near the leaded window and the telephone?

Well, nothing's defined by the keenest mind
aware of inviolate odours in halls.

Arcane, unparaphrasable halls.

Lady in distress

All this Victorian complaint of 'betrayed',
and 'vows broken' – somehow like the ribbon in your
  hair;
yet gazing into vulnerable eyes I fade
into silence. You have such an old-fashioned air.

Even your lace handkerchief, its decorous scent
of lavender, reminds of gentlewomen in hooped
  skirts;
perhaps bluff, hooting strangers would comment,
but because I do not, you appear more hurt.

Beauty dated, gilt framed, still you 'bare your heart',
unconsciously pose for a painting called Remorse.
I cannot, without offending you, depart. (Can not)
as you sigh about 'the children' and 'divorce'.

Dear, disinterested assertions are not wrong
only irrelevant as a lady's hat.
Pity, too, like a soft voice or loaded song
may confuse and confound, make a mock of it.

Some seem compassionate, some merely tough,
some cry, This is not love for love is not like this,
but since no man can ever know enough
all advice is prejudice.

On the beach

HELEN: *I never went to Troy. Only a phantom went.*
MESSENGER: *What's this? All that suffering for nothing, simply for a cloud?* [*Helena* Euripides]

Yawning, I fold yesterday's newspaper
from England, and its news of Vietnam
which has had, and will have, a thousand names.
Then I lie back on the tourist sand.

Between the sun and the sea,
far from the sun and nearer to the sea,
a cloud, a single cloud, perhaps
a cloud by Zeus planted,
not much higher than those mountains.
A cloud or a woman's face?

A cloud. Helen never came to Troy.
Mad Paris kissed the pillow where she was not,
straddled the phantom he thought he saw,
and soiling the sheets, lay back still jerking,
'Helen, Helen,' satisfied.

I rise. I am level with the haunted sea,
now clear and unclear too deep for wine,
that breathes, because of the cloud, in shadow.
It wrinkles gradually towards me.
Surprise – in the débris of near waves breaking,
deluded voices sound within its sound.

As if two, clad like Trojan women,
curse Helen – not sick Paris and his cloud.
For Hector is dead and this one is his mother,
for Hector is dead and that one is his wife,
and his babe, alive, is being torn by beasts.

No camera clicks, no front-page photograph,
no great interview. I laugh aloud,
and hear nearby a transistor braying.
Altered by its dance tune, wrongly I translate:
'Helen, Helen, where are you?
Except for that cloud the sky is blue.'

Later, I walk back to the hotel thinking:
wherever women crouch beside their dead,
as Hecuba did, as Andromache,
motionless as sculpture till they raise their head,
with mouths wildly open to howl and curse,
now they call that cloud not Helen, no,
but a thousand names, and each one still untrue.

Again I gaze beyond the mountains' range.
In depths below the sun the cloud floats through,
soundless, around the world, it seems, forever.
I go into the hotel, and change.

Pathology of colours

I know the colour rose, and it is lovely,
but not when it ripens in a tumour;
and healing greens, leaves and grass, so springlike,
in limbs that fester are not springlike.

I have seen red-blue tinged with hirsute mauve
in the plum-skin face of a suicide.
I have seen white, china white almost, stare
from behind the smashed windscreen of a car.

And the criminal, multi-coloured flash
of an H-bomb is no more beautiful
than an autopsy when the belly's opened –
to show cathedral windows never opened.

So in the simple blessing of a rainbow,
in the bevelled edge of a sunlit mirror,
I have seen, visible, Death's artifact
like a soldier's ribbon on a tunic tacked.

The sheds

Articulate suffering may be a self-admiring,
but what of the long sheds where a man could only
  howl?
How quickly, then, silhouettes came running
across the evening fields, knee deep in mist.

Or what of nights when the sheds disappeared,
fields empty, a night landscape unrhetorical
until the moon, as pale as pain, holed a cloud?
As if men slept, dreamed, as others touched on lights.

A winter convalescence

The coast shrugs, when the camera clicks,
deliberately. The cliffs blur,
and the sun's mashed in the west.

Its sac's broken, its egg-mess sticks
on the winter sea, smears it.
The air develops ghosts of soot
that become more evident, minute by minute.
They're clever. They have no shape.
Things hum.

Very few oblongs blaze
in the Grand Hotel.
God, how the promenade's empty.
The pier's empty too
but for the figure at the far end, shadowy,
hunched with a bending rod.
That one no taller than a thumb.

It's strange the way people go smaller
the further they are away. Most of the time
you even forget who died.
But supposing things did not get smaller?
Best to go inside. Best to push
revolving doors to where it's warmer,
where only a carpet makes you dizzy.

Inside, things hum.
Inside the insides the corridors wait.
A door opens, a hand comes out,
it's cut off at the elbow,
it holds a pair of shoes
cut off at the ankles.

Walk faster. God, someone is breathing,
walk faster. Humankind
cannot bear very much unreality.

That's right – lock this door, you clumsy . . .
Yet things still hum, things still hum.
Who blinks?
Who spies with his little eye
what no-one else has spied?
Best to pull the curtains on the night,
but then certain objects focus near:
the wardrobe with its narrow door,
the bible by the bedside.

Lie down, easy; lie down.
Who masturbated here?
Who whipped the ceilings? Cracked them?
Things hum.
Two blue, astringent eyes drag down their lids.
The dark comes from the lift-shaft.

Hunt the thimble

Hush now. You cannot describe it.

Is it like heavy rain falling,
and lights going on, across the fields,
in the new housing estate?

Cold, cold. Too domestic, too
temperate, too devoid of history.

Is it like a dark windowed street at night,
the houses uncurtained, the street deserted?

Colder. You are getting colder,
and too romantic, too dream-like.
You cannot describe it.

The brooding darkness then,
that breeds inside a cathedral
of a provincial town in Spain?

In Spain, also, but not Spanish.
In England, if you like, but not English.
It remains, even when obscure, perpetually.
Aged, but ageless, you cannot describe it.
No, you are cold, altogether too cold.

Aha – the blue sky over Ampourias,
the blue sky over Lancashire for that matter . . .

You cannot describe it.

. . . obscured by clouds?
I must know what you mean.

Hush, hush.

Like those old men in hospital dying,
who, unaware strangers stand around their bed,
stare obscurely, for a long moment,
at one of their own hands raised –
which perhaps is bigger than the moon again –
and then, drowsy, wandering, shout out, 'Mama'.

Is it like that? Or hours after that even:
the darkness inside a dead man's mouth?

No, no, I have told you:
you are cold, and you cannot describe it.

3 a.m. in Golders Green Road

Outside this church: TRUST IN THE LORD.
Outside that office: SAVE AND PROSPER.
Now, despite the pressures of common sense,
in this High Street before the waking time,
I think Virgil could take me by the hand
past this butcher's shop, and show me, on the hooks,
two live heads, one gnawing at the other.
I think it must be always 3 a.m. in hell.
Listen! The cenotaph clock punishes the hour –
then the strokes of silence like a horror.

The perceptible wind is immortal.
Mourning for no-one, it mourns for everyone,
it blows these damp pavements beneath the bridge
past orange belishas that blink for no-one.
There's nothing beyond but the fabric of night,
there's nothing behind but the cenotaph,
the god of this hour. It seems the tenants
afraid, left hurriedly, forgot switches,
so that occasional shop windows blaze out,
and each lamp-post, like an idiot, stares at no-one.

When rain washed cheap green from these traffic
lights
the ground smudged. My feet shake off too much
noise.
For miles around, neighbouring dogs are muzzled.
Down side-lanes, the houses darkly slumber.
The wind creaks again. Deathly crepitations
from flowered tributes to the cenotaph
on which are carved LOYALTY and JUSTICE.
Look how that god, for Time's sake, unappeased,
contemplates through its yellow monocle
all that it now owns, blankly hating it.

A night out

Friends recommended the new Polish film
at the Academy in Oxford Street.
So we joined the ever melancholy queue
of cinemas. A wind blew faint suggestions
of rain towards us, and an accordion.
Later, uneasy, in the velvet dark
we peered through the cut-out oblong window
at the spotlit drama of our nightmares:
images of Auschwitz almost authentic,
the human obscenity in close-up.
Certainly we could imagine the stench.

Resenting it, we forgot the barbed wire
was but a prop and could not scratch an eye;
those striped victims merely actors like us.
We saw the Camp orchestra assembled,
we heard the solemn gaiety of Bach,
scored by the loud arrival of an engine,
its impotent cry, and its guttural trucks.
We watched, as we munched milk chocolate,
trustful children, no older than our own,
strolling into the chambers without fuss,
while smoke, black and curly, oozed from chimneys.

Afterwards, at a loss, we sipped coffee
in a bored espresso bar nearby
saying very little. You took off one glove.
Then to the comfortable suburb swiftly
where, arriving home, we garaged the car.
We asked the au pair girl from Germany
if anyone had phoned at all, or called,
and, of course, if the children had woken.
Reassured, together we climbed the stairs,
undressed together, and naked together,
in the dark, in the marital bed, made love.

Interior

A man. A Scandinavian, coloured chair
six feet away from the television –
an advertisement, the News, an old song.
The switch, like a sponge, wipes off the picture,
and only a small, silver blob of light,
the size of anger, lingers on the screen,
then fades, to leave behind a blank oblong.

Fah

Not to irritate him did you sit,
frequenting one note, at the piano stool,
over and over; resting your finger
on that one sound till that sound vanished.
Yes, you played it again after it faded,
then felt it again and played it again
as he became anxious, a tightening nerve.

For that one sound, at first amiable,
soon touched down on the whole feminine,
far world of hermetic lamentations.
You sat there, it seemed, absent, unaware,
like a child (certainly without menace)
and fathomed it again and played it again,
a small desperation this side of death.

Not to confront him with choices
did you play: he did not quit the room quietly;
he did not shout out abruptly, 'Stop it';
he would not say with compassion, 'My dear . . .';
but only coughed behind his hand politely.
Odd, then, that he coughed again and again,
and could not stop although the tears came.

Even

Coffee-time morning, down the gradient,
like a shop window for Jehovah,
they pass my gate to the synagogue
as Saturday skies vault over.

Dressed like that they lose their charm
who carry prayer books, wear a hat.
I don't like them, I don't like them,
and guilty fret – just thinking that.

I don't like them, I don't like them –
again the dodgy thought comes through:
could it be I am another
tormented, anti-semite Jew?

No. Next morning on the Sunday,
processions uphill, piebald, lurch,
in the opposite direction,
towards the ivy-covered church.

Look, dressed for Christ and hygiene,
they glare back like Swiss-Germans
spruced and starched in piety,
and fag on slow as sermons.

All God's robots lose their charm
who carry prayer books, wear a hat.
I don't like them, I don't like them,
and feel less guilty thinking that.

So let both ministers propound
the pathology of religions,
and pass my gate you zealots of
scrubbed, excremental visions.

The ballad of Oedipus Sex

I pull the knife out of my chest,
the light begins to fail.
Don't read the Sunday papers:
myself will tell the tale.
Forget the printed photograph
that makes me look a freak.
Oedipus wrote the headlines
for longer than a week,

singing hey diddle diddlio,
hey diddle diddle dee.

It was midnight on the river,
the sky a domino.
I pushed my gloomy father
into gloomy coils below.
Such a silence on the river,
you could hear the oars creak.
Oedipus wrote the headlines
for longer than a week,

singing hey diddle diddlio,
hey diddle diddle dee.

I rowed straight home to stepmother
and seized her in my bed.
A moth was in the lampshade,
the light was in my head:
some like girls contemporary
but I like them antique.
Oedipus wrote the headlines
for longer than a week,

singing etc.

When, dripping, the ghost of father,
a hatchet in his hand,
appeared on the threshold
I found I couldn't stand;
though true love may last forever
for me it turned out bleak.
Oedipus wrote the headlines
for longer than a week,

singing etc.

I telephoned the analyst
  and conned him for a date.
 He listened to my dreaming,
  a father surrogate.
I arose and cut his throat then
  from bloody cheek to cheek.
 Oedipus wrote the headlines
  for longer than a week,

   singing etc.

The analyst had a lady,
  she never said a word;
 for when I gazed into her eyes
  a transference occurred.
So I took her to the river
  and now she's up the creek.
 Oedipus wrote the headlines
  for longer than a week,

   singing etc.

Six policemen came a-knocking,
  the door they tried to force.
 I'd have horsewhipped the lot if
  I'd only had a horse.
Six bullets through the keyhole,
  six policemen sprung a leak.
 Oedipus wrote the headlines
  for longer than a week,

   singing etc.

I was sheltered by Jocasta,
        a widow with catarrh.
    'Your sins be white as snow,' she thrilled,
        'Long as you love your ma.
Forget your past, my pet, my poodle,
        and let me be your peke.'
    Oedipus wrote the headlines
        for longer than a week,

            singing etc.

So of Jocasta now I sing
        like any swooning bard:
    the very wrinkles of her face,
        her arteries so hard.
Mock if you must! You don't know her!
        Or her veteran's technique.
    Oedipus wrote the headlines
        for longer than a week,

            singing etc.

A son we had and loved him,
        I loved him more than best;
    but on his thirteenth birthday
        he knifed me in the chest.
At the Golden Cock in Fleet Street
        they tell how Greek met Greek.
    Oedipus wrote the headlines
        for longer than a week,

            singing etc.

Since Sophocles and Shakespeare
divined our human laws,
I've gone bleeding down the aisles
to inTERminable applause.
Now I'm dying, Jocasta, dying,
my plot was not unique:
Oedipus wrote the headlines
for longer than a week,

singing hey diddle diddlio,
hey diddle diddle . . . Dada?

A suburban episode

Since you telephoned to say – in a tiny voice –
(how servile you are) intruders intruders walk
in pairs across the back lawn (I'm sorry, you say)
I say heartily, too heartily perhaps,
do not lock yourself in oh dear no,
go out, shout, challenge them, ask them why.

Since you say that some – the most impertinent –
and therefore you think (wrongly) the most
 important,
for instance, those in plum-coloured blazers,
are cutting down your tulips, snip snip snip,
one by one with small scissors, small nail-scissors,
I say with formidable aggression
stride out, ask them for credentials, stop them;
but remember walk with very long steps.

Still that is not your nature (you *are* pitiful)
and rightly you remind me you are a stranger
in this city. As for me, well you know my name,
all ratepayers know my name. I am important,
I am Vice-Chairman of the Watch Committee,
so wait for me, I say, we'll tackle them together.

So later, together, I who have been decorated
by the Queen, and you poor, timid foreigner,
swing back the door. (Whistling a merry tune
it was I, naturally, who turned the rusty key).
But, alas, there are no intruders on your lawn
nor tulips growing either, scathed or unscathed.

A tree, crashing, catapults a bird as we stand
conspiratorially together in the dusk,
you fiddling with your spectacles, and I
just one inch above the lawn, exactly one inch, I say.
And there were intruders here you say,
and there were tulips there you say.

Do not apologize. For believe me
I believe you. I know your nation (I mean your
nature)
and how cunning things can be, damnably cunning.
Why, have I not heard, even I, first cousin
of the mayor, heard in the night a stone falling?
No ordinary stone either, scraping the sheer ledges,
and later many stones, boulders even, leaping down
out of earshot, down the sides of hell.

Not Adlestrop

Not Adlestrop, no – besides, the name
hardly matters. Nor did I languish in June heat.
Simply, I stood, too early, on the empty platform,
and the wrong train came in slowly, surprised,
stopped.
Directly facing me, from a window,
a very, *very* pretty girl leaned out.

When I, all instinct,
stared at her, she, all instinct, inclined her head away
as if she'd divined the much married life in me,
or as if she might spot, up platform,
some unlikely familiar.

For my part, under the clock, I continued
my scrutiny with unmitigated pleasure.
And she knew it, she certainly knew it, and would
not
glance at me in the silence of not Adlestrop.

Only when the train heaved noisily, only
when it jolted, when it slid away, only *then*,
daring and secure, she smiled back at my smile,
and I, daring and secure, waved back at her waving.
And so it was, all the way down the hurrying
platform
as the train gathered atrocious speed
towards Oxfordshire or Gloucestershire.

In Llandough Hospital

'To hasten night would be humane,'
I, a doctor, beg a doctor,
for still the darkness will not come –
his sunset slow, his first star pain.

I plead: 'We know another law.
For one maimed bird we'd do as much,
and if a creature need not suffer
must he, for etiquette, endure?'

Earlier, 'Go now, son,' my father said,
for my sake commanding me.
Now, since death makes victims of us all,
he's thin as Auschwitz in that bed.

Still his courage startles me. The fears
I'd have, he has none. Who'd save
Socrates from the hemlock,
or Winkelried from the spears?

We quote or misquote in defeat,
in life, and at the camps of death.
Here comes the night with all its stars,
bright butchers' hooks for man and meat.

I grasp his hand so fine, so mild,
which still is warm surprisingly,
not a handshake either, father,
but as I used to when a child.

And as a child can't comprehend
what germinates philosophy,
so like a child I question why
night with stars, then night without end.

Two small stones

After the therapy of the grave ritual
(mourners who weep circumspectly weep less long)
'A fine man.' No-one snarled the priest was wrong.
Relatives pressed limp hands, filed out, heads bowed,
emotional as opera singers. But mute their song.

I do not know why I picked up two small stones
(bits of broken sky trailed on the gravel path)
and dropped them in my pocket. No epitaph,
no valediction pardoned me. Why didn't I cry,
and why won't I throw these stones away? Don't
   laugh.

Not beautiful

In all hiroshimas, in raw and raving voices,
   live skeletons of the Camp, flies hugging faeces,
      in war, in famine, he'd find the beautiful.

Being saintly, his vocation was to find it
   at the dying bedside, in the disrobing dead.
      And what he did, they said, you should be trying.

Well, once, while dissecting a nerve in a cadaver
   my cigarette dropped, fell into its abdomen.
      I picked it up. I puffed out the smoke of hell.

Yet still was not fit for time to come: the freehold grave,
things run over like slush all bloody and throbbing –
for though they were dumb, not beautiful, I said.

It's the parable again of the three wise men:
the first who, with finger and thumb, tweaked his nostrils,
and the second who pressed his eyes to his palms,

whilst the third, the wisest, cried, 'Oh what beautiful,
white teeth have these vermin which died.' Homo sum,
etc., but the third was divine (as they said).

One sees the good point, of course, and may admire it;
but, sometimes, I think that to curse is more sacred
than to pretend by affirming. And offend.

Interview with a spirit healer

Smiling, he says no man should fear the tomb
for where we fade the grass is greener.
Listen! Someone coughs in his waiting room;
then, from upstairs, the suburban howl of
the made ghost in a vacuum cleaner.

With nude emotion, he names the miracles
as hip fans would football matches.
His voice catches on the incurably cured
whose letters, testimonials, conclude,
'. . . though the doctors gave me up as hopeless'.

His tragic venue, those frayed English spas:
Cheltenham, Leamington, Tunbridge, Bath,
where depressed male Tories, on their sticks,
guzzle in chromium and maroon hotel bars
which seem more empty when people whisper.

He murmurs, 'Love,' which could be disturbing,
also 'Spirit guides.' Look, his upraised hand
shows me neither its knuckles nor its palm,
and, like a candle in daytime burning,
seems but a sign ethereal as a psalm.

Goodbye! His spirituality is too inbred,
too indelible like a watermark;
and I, gross sceptic, hired by a paper,
prefer my dead to be in the dark.
Goodbye. His eyes, Mary's blue, stare at vapour.

Let him, in faith, stare on. I loathe his trade,
the disease and the sanctimonious lie
that cannot cure the disease. My need,
being healthy, is not faith; but to curse the day
I became mortal the night my father died.

Give me your hands

Scared trees, hissing in the garden,
can't hear human voices harden.
I can: my two neighbours quarrel.

Mine ! Mine! Nothing to do with me.
Once more I flex my head to see
the latest Sunday photograph.

In Vietnam, beneath scarred trees,
unreal the staring casualties.
Of course I care. What good is that?

Faint in the hall the telephone goes.
As I approach, how loud it grows.
I lift up a voice saying, 'Doctor?'

So in a room I do not know
I hold a hand I do not know
for hours. Again a dry old hand.

There's something else that I must do,
for some other thing is crying too
in chaos, near, without a name.

Remembering Miguel Hernandez

The noise of many knuckles on metal,
we do not hear it.
There is lightning when we are asleep
and thunder that does not speak;
there are guitars without strings
and nightingales with tongues of glass.

Yet even if we imagine it,
the metal sound of bolts shut to,
then feet stamping down echoing corridors,
what can we do who stroll on easy grass,
who smile back at the gracious and the goodlooking?

Righteous the rhetoric of indignation,
but protesting poems, like the plaster angels,
are impotent. They commit no crimes,
they pass no laws; they grant amnesty
only to those who, in safety, write them.

The nameless

There is the eight hour sleep and the forgetting,
and the leaving behind: the nameless things,
or rather the unnameable – cries in the back lane,
the closing of a frosted windowpane.
Yes, to reach for the unidentifiable
we list such details; it seems we're unable
to exorcize, or diminish, or claim
what arrives, at desolate moments, home.

And even music is memory that has faded.

Still we categorize: a key turning round a lock,
the odour in a public telephone box,
or certain tunes with their measured malice
that remind us of the dead; the abyss
below everything, a hole in the eye,
a hole in the earth, a hole in the memory,
and we are called, though our names are not ours
till carved on the gravestone for hours and hours.

Anonymities

I

Christ, a spaceman, diving *up*,
head first to heaven – crazy, absurd,
even though painted by Titian.

Outside the Palace of the Dukes
the dying beggar of Urbino
accosted us.

His blue, aryan eye surprised us.
He was offensive, having no name.

2

At Gradara, perhaps,
even Paolo and Francesca
would walk in their electric ghosts,
pace the battlements, twice nightly,
though I saw no advertisement.

A mile down the road from the castle,
before the level crossing, look!
. . . the war cemetery.
No ghost would stir there being nameless.
I held my dark glasses in my hand;
the air, therefore, no longer khaki.

What a real green prettiness
devised poppies not made of paper.
Silence seemed obligatory.
Afterwards, I pulled the starter three times:
the usual choking noise of an imbecile
before the car edged forward.

My sun-glasses now back in front of my eyes,
I thought: 'Soldier . . . soldiers . . .
don't you know yet? Your uniform even . . .
Khaki is the colour of shit . . .'

3

At 4 o'clock on the autostrada,
hot, very hot, and far to the left the mountains,
somewhere between Bologna and Milan,
cars unreeled in a fragmented,
rising and fading hysteria.

It happened then:

a squealing, a destroying noise
through the khaki afternoon.
Coming towards us from the other side
a car was heaving into pieces,
through air undulating like cheap glass,
lancinating metal flying
across the road, lasciviously.

But, 'Press on,' I thought, and swerved
in the buckled sunlight to avoid another car
which in decent mercy had braked in front.
'Cool,' I thought, 'I am cool in a crisis,'
feeling proud, omnipotent, self-absorbed.

Later, of course, grew ashamed when '*Kaput*'
said the ambulance man, having no English.
Now we peered through real glass that was flawed.
One eye, blue as Urbino, could not blink;
as for the other, not an eye at all
but the material of a poppy.
And flies sat on the meat.

4

In Milan, next morning, I, a tourist,
visited 'the wedding cake' cathedral,
and felt nothing.
All that vain, perpendicular magnificence,
that yearning melodrama of glass and stone,
how it towered, how it strained,
but, of course, could not fly to heaven.
I felt nothing.

For 200 lire, on the vertigo of its roofs,
other tourists also clambered.
Amongst the monstrous gargoyles I laughed,
raggedly,
and said, with the genius of an idiot,
'What a wedding cake when the bride is Death!'

Down, down, angled down below,
on the square, the smallest people ever
scurried ridiculously.
I blinked from a large, ceremonial eye.
With a long leg, my shoe could have stamped one
out.
It wouldn't have mattered.
Not knowing whom.

The motto

Who heard the no thing to write nothing down?
Who switched the record player on instead?

Whose slate-blue smoke idled to the lampshade?
Who killed his cigarette and went to bed?

Who, half the night, could not sleep for Mozart
And thought to hell with all those classic gems?

Who said without such music in the head
A man's more fit for stratagems?

He bungled though – when music sought him out.
He whistled still, but did not know what for.

His stick in winter doodled in the snow:
Be visited, expect nothing, and endure.

The smile was

one thing I waited for always
after the shouting
after the palaver
the perineum stretched to pain
the parched voice of the midwife
                    Push! Push!

and I can't and the rank
sweet smell of the gas
and
                              I can't
as she whiffed cotton wool
inside her head
as the hollow stones of gas
dragged
                    her
                         down
from the lights above
to the river-bed, to the real stones.
                              Push! Push!
as she floated up again
muscles tensed, to the electric
till the little head was crowned;
and I shall wait again
for the affirmation.

For it is such:
that effulgent, tender, satisfied
smile of a woman
who, for the first time,
hears the child crying the world
for the very first time.

That agreeable, radiant smile –
no man can smile it
no man can paint it
as it develops without fail,
after the gross, physical, knotted,
granular, bloody endeavour.
   Such a pure spirituality, from all that!
It occupies the face
and commands it.
                        Out of relief
you say, reasonably thinking of the reasonable,
swinging lightness of any reprieve,
the joy of it, almost helium in the head.

                        So wouldn't you?
And truly there's always the torture of the unknown.
There's always the dream of pregnant women,
blood of the monster in the blood of the child;
and we all know of generations lost
like words faded on a stone,
of minds blank or wild with genetic mud.
                        And couldn't you
smile like that?

Not like that, no, never,
not with such indefinable
dulcitude as that.
And so she smiles
with eyes as brown as a dog's
or eyes blue-mad as a doll's
it makes no odds
whore, beauty, or bitch,
it makes no odds
illimitable chaste happiness
in that smile
as new life-in-the-world
for the first time cries the world.
No man can smile like that.

2

No man can paint it.
Da Vinci sought it out
yet was far, far, hopelessly.
Leonardo, you only made
Mona Lisa look six months gone!

I remember the smile of the Indian.
I told him
                    Fine, finished,
you are cured
and he sat there smiling sadly.
Any painter could paint it
the smile of a man resigned
saying
                    Thank you, doctor,
you have been kind
and then, as in melodrama,
                    How long
have I to live?
The Indian smiling, resigned,
all the fatalism of the East.

So one starts again, also smiling,
                    All is well
you are well, you are cured.
And the Indian still smiling
his assignations with death
still shaking his head, resigned.
                    Thank you
for telling me the truth, doctor.
Two months? Three months?

And beginning again
  and again
whatever I said, thumping the table,
however much I reassured him
the more he smiled the conspiratorial
smile of a damned, doomed man.

Now a woman, a lady, a whore,
a bitch, a beauty, whatever,
  the child's face crumpled
as she becomes the mother
she smiles differently, ineffably.

3

As different as
the smile of my colleague,
his eyes reveal it,
his ambiguous assignations,
good man, good surgeon,
whose smile arrives of its own accord
  from nowhere
like flies to a dead thing
when he makes the first incision.

Who draws a line of blood
across the soft, white flesh
as if something beneath,
desiring violence, had beckoned him;
who draws a ritual wound,
a calculated wound
to heal – to heal,
but still a wound –
good man, good surgeon,
his smile as luxuriant
as the smile of Peter Lorre.

So is the smile of my colleague,
the smile of a man
secretive behind the mask.

The smile of war.

But the smile, the smile
of the new mother,
what
        an extraordinary
                open thing
                        it is.

4

Walking home tonight I saw
an ordinary occurrence
hardly worth remarking on:
an unhinged star, a streaking gas,
and I thought how lovely
destruction is when it is far.
Ruined it slid
on the dead dark towards fiction:
its lit world disappeared
phut, through one punched hole or another,
slipped unseen down the back of the sky
into another time.

Never,
not for one single death
can I forget we die with the dead,
and the world dies with us;
yet
in one, lonely,
small child's birth
all the tall dead rise
to break the crust of the imperative earth.

No wonder the mother smiles
a wonder like that,
a lady, a whore, a bitch, a beauty.
Eve smiled like that
when she heard Seth cry out Abel's dark,
earth dark, the first dark
eeling on the deep sea-bed,
struggling on the real stones.
Hecuba, Cleopatra, Lucretia Borgia,
Annette Vallon smiled like that.

They all, still, smile like that,
when the child first whimpers like a seagull
the ancient smile reasserts itself
instinct with a return
so outrageous and so shameless;
the smile the smile
always the same
                    an uncaging
                      a freedom.

Mysteries

At night, I do not know who I am
when I dream, when I am sleeping.

Awakened, I hold my breath and listen:
a thumbnail scratches the other side of the wall.

At midday, I enter a sunlit room
to observe the lamplight on for no reason.

I should know by now that few octaves can be heard,
that a vision dies from being too long stared at;

that the whole of recorded history even
is but a little gossip in a great silence;

that a magnesium flash cannot illumine,
for one single moment, the invisible.

I do not complain. I start with the visible
and am startled by the visible.

Forgotten

That old country I once said I'd visit
when older. Can no one tell me its name?
Odd, to have forgotten what it is called.
I would recognize the name if I heard it.
So many times I have searched the atlas
with a prowling convex lens – to no avail.

I know the geography of the great world
has changed; the war, the peace, the deletions
of places – red pieces gone forever,
and names of countries altered forever:
Gold Coast Ghana, Persia become Iran,
Siam Thailand, and Hell now Vietnam.

People deleted. Must I sleep again to reach it,
to find the back door opening to a field,
a barking of dogs, and a path that leads back?
One night in pain, the dead middle of night,
will I awake again, know who I am,
the man from somewhere else, and the place's name?

An old commitment

Long ago my kinsmen slain in battle,
swart flies on all their pale masks feeding.

I had a cause then. Surely I had a cause?
I was for them and they were for me.

Now, when I recall why, what, who,
I think the thought that is as blank as stone.

Travelling this evening, I focus on the back
of brightness, on that red spot wavering.

Behind it, what have I forgotten? It goes
where the red spot goes, rising, descending.

I only describe a sunset, a car travelling
on a swerving mountain road, that's all.

Arriving too late, I approach the unlit dark.
Those who loiter outside exits and entrances

so sadly, so patiently, even they have departed.
And I am no ghost and this place is in ruins.

'Black,' I call softly to one dead but beloved,
'black, black,' wanting the night to reply . . .

. . . 'Black.'

Demo against the Vietnam war, 1968

Praise just one thing in London, he challenged,
as if everybody, everything, owned a minus,
was damnable, and the Inner Circle led to hell;
and I thought, allowed one slot only,
what, in October, would I choose?

Not the blurred grasslands of a royal, moody park
where great classy trees lurk in mist;
not the secretive Thames either, silvering
its slow knots through the East End –
sooty scenes, good for Antonioni panning soft
atmospheric shots, emblems of isolation,
prologue to the elegiac Square, the house where,
suddenly, lemon oblongs spring to windows.

Nor would I choose the stylized catalogue
of torment in the National Gallery.
Better that tatty group, under Nelson's column,
their home-made banners held aloft,
their small cries of 'Peace, Peace,' impotent;
also the moment with the tannoy turned off,
the thudding wings of pigeons audible,
the shredding fountains, once again, audible.

So praise to the end of the march,
their songs, their jargon, outside the Embassy.
Yes, this I'd choose: their ardour, their naïveté,
violence of commitment, cruelty of devotion,
'We shall not be moved, We shall overcome' –
despite sullen police concealed in vans
waiting for arclights to fail, for furtive darkness,
and camera-teams, dismantled, all breezing home.

Haloes

Of course haloes are out of fashion.
The commissar is in the castle,
the haemophylic king plays golf
in exile. Feudal days, no more.
Once martyrs were a glut on the market,
now famine faces sink in Asia;
now lamps switched on in drawing rooms
reveal suffering saints no longer there –
as if they had leapt down from walls
leaving behind them halo-tissue.

Such a round shining on walls!
Such a bleeding of intense light!
And all those haloes in hymns of paint,
in museums, in galleries, counterfeit.
Still we appease the old deities –
else we would be like madmen laughing
in public buildings, apparent joy
where rational people speak in whispers;
else saints would never look so ecstatic
in chiaroscuro, on starvation diet.

The Pope does not eat his own entrails
with a golden fork, nor his secretary
cease from phoning the Stock Exchange.
Haloes set men alight in Prague.
Here crowds prefer to shout, 'Easy, Easy,'
at a poisoned green pitch in floodlight.
Pop star, film star, space man, gangster,
move smilingly from camera to camera
seldom to become ritual torches.
Each worth a million, say the guides.

Rightly we are suspicious of haloes
and heroes, of thorns and royal tiaras.
Day and night, an H-bomb circles the world
and Fatty and his henchmen walk
on marble floors, their heritage.
No wonder important men lift up
their hats politely, revealing bald heads.
No-one minds. Their skins have healed.
Think of wall lamps switched off
savagely, all haloes fleeing.

Moon object

After the astronaut's intrusion of moonlight, after
the metal flag, the computer-speeches – this little booty.

Is it really from the moon? Identify it if you can.
Test it, blue-eyed scientist, between finger and thumb.

Through a rainy city a car continues numb.
Its radio blanks out beneath a bridge.

In a restaurant, your colleague with a cold
is trying to taste his own saliva.

On the school piano, your wife's index finger
sinks the highest note. She hears the sound of felt.

Blue eyes, let your own finger and your thumb
slip and slide about it devilishly.

Don't you feel the gravity of the moon?
Say a prayer for the dead and murmur a vow.

Change your white coat for a purple cloak
and cage yourself a peacock or a gnat.

No, rational, you sniff it. But some holes in your front-brain
have been scooped out. A moon-howling dog would know.

Blue eyes, observe it again. See its dull appearance
and be careful: it could be cursed, it could be sleeping.

Awake, it might change colour like a lampshade
turned on, seething – suddenly moon-plugged.

Scientist, something rum has happened to you.
Your right and left eyes have been switched around.

Back home, if you dialled your own number now,
a shameless voice would reply, 'Who? Who?'

Peachstone

I do not visit his grave. He is not there.
Out of hearing, out of reach. I miss him here,
seeing hair grease at the back of a chair
near a firegrate where his spit sizzled,
or noting, in the cut-glass bowl, a peach.

For that night his wife brought him a peach,
his favourite fruit, while the sick light glowed,
and his slack, dry mouth sucked, sucked, sucked,
with dying eyes closed – perhaps for her sake –
till bright as blood the peachstone showed.

Three street musicians

Three street musicians in mourning overcoats
worn too long, shake money boxes this morning,
then, afterwards, play their suicide notes.

The violinist in chic, black spectacles, blind,
the stout tenor with a fake Napoleon stance,
and the loony flautist following behind,

they try to importune us, the busy living,
who hear melodic snatches of music hall
above unceasing waterfalls of traffic.

Yet if anything can summon back the dead
it is the old-time sound, old obstinate tunes,
such as they achingly render and suspend:

'The Minstrel Boy', 'Roses of Picardy'.
No wonder cemeteries are full of silences
and stones keep down the dead that they defend.

Stones too light! Airs irresistible!
Even a dog listens, one paw raised, while the stout,
loud man amazes with nostalgic notes – though half
boozed

and half clapped out. And, as breadcrumbs thrown
on the ground charm sparrows down from nowhere,
now, suddenly, there are too many ghosts about.

Portrait of the artist as a middle-aged man

(*3.30 a.m., January 1st*)

Pure Xmas card below – street under snow,
under lamplight. My children curl asleep,
my wife also moans from depths too deep
with all her shutters closed and half her life.
And I? I, sober now, come down the stairs
to eat an apple, to taste the snow in it,
to switch the light on at the maudlin time.

Habitual living room, where the apple-flesh
turns brown after the bite, oh half my life
has gone to pot. And, now, too tired for sleep,
I count up the Xmas cards childishly,
assessing, *Jesus*, how many friends I've got!

A new diary

This clerk-work, this first January chore
of who's in, who's out. A list to think about
when absences seem to shout, Scandal! Outrage!
So turning to the blank, prefatory page
I transfer most of the names and phone tags
from last year's diary. True, Meadway, Speedwell,
Mountview, are computer-changed into numbers,
and already their pretty names begin to fade
like Morwenna, Julie, Don't-Forget-Me-Kate,
grassy summer girls I once swore love to.
These, whispering others and time will date.

Cancelled, too, a couple someone else betrayed,
one man dying, another mind in rags.
And remembering them my clerk-work flags,
bitterly flags, for all lose, no-one wins,
those in, those out, *this* at the heart of things.
So I stop, ask: whom should I commemorate,
and who, perhaps, is crossing out my name now
from some future diary? Oh my God,
Morwenna, Julie, don't forget me, Kate.

Miss Book World

We, the judges, a literary lot,
peep-tom legitimately at these beauties,
give marks for legs and breasts, make remarks
low or pompous like most celebrities;
not that we are, but they imagine us so
who parade blatantly as camera-lights flash
crazily for a glossy page and cash.

Perhaps some girls entered for a giggle,
but all walk slave-like in this ritual fuss
of unfunny compère, funny applause,
spotlit dream-girls displayed, a harem for us;
not that they are, but we imagine them so,
with Miss Book World herself just barely flawed,
almost perfect woman, almost perfect fraud.

The illusion over, half the contestants
still fancy themselves in their knock-out pose,
while we literati return to the real
world of fancy, great poetry and prose;
not that it is, but we imagine it so,
great vacant visions in which we delight,
as if we see the stars not only at night.

The death of Aunt Alice

Aunt Alice's funeral was orderly,
each mourner correct, dressed in decent black,
not one balding relative berserk with an axe.
Poor Alice, where's your opera-ending?
For alive you relished high catastrophe,
your bible Page One of a newspaper.

You talked of typhoid when we sat to eat;
Fords on the M4, mangled, upside down,
just when we were going for a spin;
and, at London airport, as you waved us off,
how you fatigued us with 'metal fatigue',
vague shapes of Boeings bubbling under seas.

Such disguises and such transformations!
Even trees were but factories for coffins,
rose bushes decoys to rip boys' eyes with thorns.
Sparrows became vampires, spiders had designs,
and your friends also grew SPECTACULAR,
none to bore you by dying naturally.

A. had both kidneys removed in error
at Guy's. 'And such a clever surgeon too.'
B., one night, fell screaming down a liftshaft.
'Poor fellow, he never had a head for heights.'
C., so witty, so feminine, 'Pity
she ended up in a concrete-mixer.'

But now, never again, Alice, will you utter
gory admonitions as some do oaths.
Disasters that lit your eyes will no more
unless, trembling up there, pale saints listen
to details of their bloody martyrdoms,
all their tall stories, your eternity.

Car journeys

I *Down the M4*

Me! dutiful son going back to South Wales, this time afraid
to hear my mother's news. Too often, now, her friends are disrobed,
and my aunts and uncles, too, go into the hole, one by one.
The beautiful face of my mother is in its ninth decade.

Each visit she tells me the monotonous story of clocks.
'Oh dear,' I say, or 'how funny,' till I feel my hair turning grey
for I've heard that perishable one two hundred times before –
like the rugby 'amateurs' with golden sovereigns in their socks.

Then the Tawe ran fluent and trout-coloured over
stones stonier,
more genuine; then Annabella, my mother's mother,
spoke Welsh
with such an accent the village said, 'Tell the truth,
fach,
you're no Jewess. *They're* from the Bible. *You're*
from Patagonia!'

I'm driving down the M4 again under bridges that
leap
over me then shrink in my side mirror. Ystalyfera is
farther
than smoke and God further than all distance known.
I whistle
no hymn but an old Yiddish tune my mother knows.
It won't keep.

2 *Incident on a summer night*

The route not even in the A.A. book.
I'm nowhere, I thought, driving slowly
because of the raw surface of the lane
that developed between converging hedges;
then, soon, fabulous in the ghastly wash
of headlights, a naked man approached
crying without inhibition, one hand to his face,
his somehow familiar mouth agape.

Surely he could see me?
From the two moth-filled headlights
surely he would draw back, change his pace?
This road to Paradise, I muttered.
At last I passed him or say, rather, he passed me.
Afterwards, the accelerating lane widened
and long lights fumbled, momentarily,
hedges, hurtling gate, country wall, amazing tree.

3 *I sit in my parked car*

And they, too, seem like images from sleep:
this Asian child and shadow
playing on a rubbish heap;
that old man incognito
preaching to the pigeons.
'Kill the Reds,' he says, 'kill the Reds.'
I wind up the car window.

Nearby, sunlight on a broken bottle
throws trinket colours on a stone,
but the ancient man in smoked glasses
walks to the right alone
mouthing a forgotten language,
walks out of sight, off the page.

And I? I leave the car, feel dizzy –
even the plastic seating's hot.
Grounded pigeons purr their gutturals,
the pistons in their heads are busy.
When the door slams its small shot
the pigeons reach for the sky,
the shadow chases the child.

In Hotel Insomnia, once, at dawn,
I thought I heard those pigeons' wings
whirring outside my numbered door.
It was only the lift gone wild.
Up and down on a nightmare ride
its gates opened at each floor,
gates of ivory or of horn:
no Asian child, nor ancient man.
nobody at all inside.

4 *Driving home*

Opposing carbeams wash my face.
Such flickerings hypnotize. To keep awake
I listen to the BBC through cracklings
of static, fade-outs under bridges,
to a cool expert who, in lower case,
computes and graphs 'the ecological
disasters that confront the human race.'

Almost immediately (ironically?),
I see blue flashing lights ahead and brake
before a car accordioned, floodlit, men heaving
at a stretcher, an ambulance oddly angled, tame, in
  wait.
Afterwards, silent, I drive home cautiously
where, late, the eyes of my youngest child
flicker dreamily, and are full of television.

'He's waited up,' his mother says, 'to say goodnight.'
My son smiles briefly. Such emotion! I surprise
myself and him when I hug him tight.

A note left on the mantelpiece

(For his wife)

Attracted by their winning names I chose
Little Yid and *Welsh Bard*; years later backed
the swanky jockeys, and still thought I lacked
inspiration, the uncommon touch, not
mere expertise. Each way, I paid in prose.

Always the colours and stadiums beckoned
till, on the nose, at Goodwood, the high gods
jinxed the favourite despite the odds.
Addict that I was, live fool and dead cert.
His velvet nostrils lagged a useless second.

A poet should have studied style not form
(sweet, I regret the scarcity of roses)
but by Moses and by the nine Muses
I'll no more. Each cruising nag is a beast
so other shirts can keep the centaur warm.

Adieu, you fading furlongs of boozing,
hoarse voices at Brighton, white rails, green course.
Conclusion? Why, not only the damned horse
but whom it's running against matters.
By the way, apologies for losing.

A faithful wife

(A letter written by an Egyptian lady during the reign of Amenhotep III, about 1385 BCE*)*

To my husband, my lord,
whose caravans lodge in Canaan,
whose sperm has not stiffened,
for three long months, my bed-linen,
say:
at the feet of my husband,
as before the king, the sun-god,
seven times and seven times
I fall.
For I am an obedient
of my husband, my lord.

When I keep my head still
moving my two eyes this way
it is dark;
when I keep my head still
moving my two eyes that way
it is dark;
but when I gaze in front,
towards my lord, it is dazzle,
it is the spirit on the wall
flat as a sunbeam:
it is the time of the short shadows.

Further: all seems tasteless
like the white of an egg
since my lord departed.
Thus ask my falcon, my husband,
to send for his servant, as promised,
to journey on the stony heat
across the camel-coloured desert
even to the shrewd wells.
For I have placed the yoke
of my husband, my lord,
upon my neck and I bear it.

In the whirling dust-storm,
a brick may move
from beneath its companions.
When the night grows with jackals
a dog may move
from his sick master.
But send for me and I shall not move
from beneath the shadow
of my husband, my lord,
as that shadow will not move
from his two feet.

Yet my lord sends no report,
neither good nor evil.
Has he gone to the land of Hatti,
or to the region of the bedouins?
Does he take care of his chariot?
When the first three stars appear
does he sleep each evening
with a piece of wool upon him?
Or has the foe raided his caravans,
the night guards drunk, my lord inert?
Very anxious is thy servant.

Oh may this tablet find him safe
in Joppa, in the meadows
blossoming in their season:
else let the dust follow his chariot
like smoke, and let the god, Amon, keep
all those tracks that zag between
the rising and the setting sun
free from ambuscade,
free for my lord whose speeches are
gathered together on my tongue,
and remain upon my lips.

Here

(For Jeremy Robson)

In the precincts of cautious Golders Green,
at a front gate, my companion and I
hardly noticed the tidy, mowed gardens
of 3 p.m., the hydrangeas, the sign
FOR SALE, a parked car in steady sunlight.
Simply, we were about to say, 'goodbye,'
when suddenly, startled, we saw unlikely
down the empty street, flouncing towards us
the ribboned horse and cart, the fat driver

solemn, outrageous, in a tall top hat,
garbed in funeral satin black – and in the cart
a brightness of balloons, a batty cargo,
slowly slowly bouncing, light as moon-air,
all the colours of a festival.
The driver did not smile, did not raise his hat,
jogging down the afternoon, going where,
deaf to our world, the afternoon must go.

Since then, 1000 afternoons have gone
unremarkably, and still I savour
its bland mystery, the oddness of it,
the unfathomable, blind, rare uses
I may make of it: that something not dreamt,
I swear I swear, something not fantasy,
not film shot – though, now, true fancy ablaze,
I see one fat reader lift his ancient eyes,
deaf to our world, and raise his tall black hat.

The bereaved

I

Once his voice had been so thrilling,
the twelve women all agreed. Off and on TV
he was charming, he was charismatic,
yet without side. He was their pin-up.

But now his incomprehensible language
when he spoke (which was rare);
the way he would stare into chasms of space
as if Eurydice were there; or would suddenly

howl out an emptiness – that was too much
(a man should not dream of maggots too long)
that was ridiculous, even frightening, they said,
the twelve women, reasonably moving towards him.

2

Twelve women pulling him,
twelve women screaming,
kicking, scratching, pulling at him,
until on the ground, at last,
he was being smothered,
bitten by women's teeth,
his eyes pushed in by women's thumbs.

Afterwards, the cyanosed figure
on the ground, what was left of him,
striped with blood, did not move,
and the women stood back silent,
most of them already smoking
and the others lighting up.

Explanation of a news item

Police Constable Appleton said, 'At eight o'clock in the morning the children looked through the railings and saw him walking slowly through the cemetery.'

He leading, they floated up
in slow motion, as if under water
(though there was no water)
to the small, bright oblong above.
'Are you ready?' he asked,
with outstretched hand blindly.
'I must not,' he heard her whisper,
'I am but a ghost, a glitter on dust
fading in the upper light.'
He did not understand: he turned,
he looked down into the dark,
he looked aghast – and suddenly
her voice plunging cried out
like an echo of an echo of an echo,
so that he awoke startled
in the February sunlight,
walking on the gravel pathway
between the stone-eyed angels
and the nicely ordered graves.

No more Mozart

High to the right a hill of trees,
a fuselage of branches,
reflects German moonlight
like dull armour.
Sieg heil!

Higher still, one moon migrates deathwards,
a white temper between clouds.
To the left, the other slides
undulating on the black
oiled, rippling reservoir.

Can't sleep for Mozart,
and on the winter glass
a shilling's worth of glitter.

The German streets tonight
are soaped in moonlight.
The streets of Germany are clean
like the hands of Lady Macbeth.

Back in bed the eyes close, do not sleep.
Achtung! Achtung!
Someone is breathing nearby,
someone not accounted for.

Now, of course, no more Mozart.
With eyes closed still
the body touches itself, takes stock.
Above the hands the thin wrists
attached to them; and on the wrists
the lampshade material.
Also the little hairs that can be pulled.

The eyes open:
the German earth is made of helmets;
the wind seeps through a deep
frost hole that is somewhere else
carrying the far Jew-sounds of railway trucks.

Nothing is annulled:
the blood vow, the undecorated cry,
someone robbed of his name,
then silence again.

Afterwards:
the needle rests on a record
with nothing on that record turning,
neither sound nor silence,
for it is sleep at last.

There, the fugitive body has arrived
at the stink of nothing.
And twelve million eyes
in six million heads
stare in the same direction.

Outside, the electrician works
inside his cloud, silently,
and the reservoir darkens.

Germany 1970

The case

From the ward's far window he stared
through the weighted trees at the tennis court,
its ground red as Devonshire, old rusted blood.
His own had been syringed, drawn off many times,
I learnt from the tall doctor, my colleague,
for sedimentation rates, white cell counts,
haemoglobin content, clotting time,
bleeding time, agglutination tests,
many blood-cultures over many months.
For the patient had been ill many months,
sometimes feeling better, out of bed,
watching the sunlight altering the lawns
or rain in the tennis court. Now, on the grass,
leaves had settled, orange brown yellow,
soaked chemically, dyed in autumn blood.
'Let me speak to your patient then,' I said,
and on the walls the sunlight fused abruptly.
'What's his name?' My colleague had not understood
who knew the man's heart but not the man.
Smiling at rows of beds we walked on

parquet floors, up the ward, and I shook hands
with a shadow. 'Good morning, John,' I said,
reading his name on the temperature chart.

Miracles

Last night, the priest dreamed he quit his church
at midnight, and then saw vividly
a rainbow in the black sky.
I said, every day, you can see
conjunctions equally odd – awake and sane, that is –
a tangerine on the snow, say.
Such things are no more incredible than God.

Such things, said the priest, do not destroy a man,
but seeing a rainbow in the night sky
– awake and sane, that is – why, doctor,
like a gunshot that could destroy a man.
That would not allow him to believe in anything,
neither to praise nor blame. A doctor must believe
in miracles, but I, a priest, dare not.

Then my incurable cancer patient,
the priest, sat up in bed, looked to the window,
and peeled his tangerine, silently.

In the theatre

(*A true incident*)

'Only a local anaesthetic was given because of the blood pressure problem. The patient, thus, was fully awake throughout the operation. But in those days – in 1938, in Cardiff, when I was Lambert Rogers' dresser – they could not locate a brain tumour with precision. Too much normal brain tissue was destroyed as the surgeon crudely searched for it, before he felt the resistance of it . . . all somewhat hit and miss. One operation I shall never forget. . . .'

(*Dr Wilfred Abse*)

Sister saying – 'Soon you'll be back in the ward,'
sister thinking – 'Only two more on the list,'
the patient saying – 'Thank you, I feel fine';
small voices, small lies, nothing untoward,
though, soon, he would blink again and again
because of the fingers of Lambert Rogers,
rash as a blind man's, inside his soft brain.

If items of horror can make a man laugh
then laugh at this: one hour later, the growth
still undiscovered, ticking its own wild time;
more brain mashed because of the probe's braille
path;
Lambert Rogers desperate, fingering still;
his dresser thinking, 'Christ! Two more on the list,
a cisternal puncture and a neural cyst.'

Then, suddenly, the cracked record in the brain,
a ventriloquist voice that cried, 'You sod,
leave my soul alone, leave my soul alone,' –
the patient's dummy lips moving to that refrain,
the patient's eyes too wide. And, shocked,
Lambert Rogers drawing out the probe
with nurses, students, sister, petrified.

'Leave my soul alone, leave my soul alone,'
that voice so arctic and that cry so odd
had nowhere else to go – till the antique
gramophone wound down and the words began
to blur and slow, '. . . leave . . . my . . . soul . . .
   alone . . .'
to cease at last when something other died.
And silence matched the silence under snow.

Funland

1 The superintendent

With considerable poise
the superintendent
has been sitting for hours now
at the polished table.

Outside the tall window
all manner of items
have been thundering down
boom boom stagily
the junk of heaven.

A harp with the nerves missing
the somewhat rusty
sheet iron wings of an angel
a small bent tubular hoop
still flickering flickering
like fluorescent lighting
when first switched on
that old tin lizzie banger
Elijah's burnt-out chariot
various other religious hardware
and to cap it all
you may not believe this
a red Edwardian pillar box.

My atheist uncle has been standing
in the corner wrathfully.
Fat Blondie in her pink
transparent nightdress
has been kneeling
on the brown linoleum.

And for some queer reason
our American guest yells
from time to time Mari-*an*
if they give you chewing gum
. . . . CHEW.

Meanwhile the superintendent
a cautious man usually
inclined for instance
to smile in millimetres
has begun to take a great risk.

Calm as usual
masterful as usual
he is drawing the plans of the void
working out its classical proportions.

2 Anybody here seen any Thracians?

The tall handsome man
whom the superintendent
has nicknamed Pythagoras
asked fat Blondie
as she reclined strategically
under the cherry blossom
to join his Society.

The day after that
despite initial fleerings
my uncle also agreed.
The day following another hundred.
Two more weeks everyone
had signed on the dotted line.

There are very few rules.
Members promise to abstain
from swallowing beans. They promise
not to pick up what has fallen
never to stir a fire with an iron
never to eat the heart of animals
never to walk on motorways
never to look in a mirror
that hangs beside a light.
All of us are happy with the rules.

But Pythagoras is not happy.
He wanted to found
a Society not a Religion
and a Society he says
washing his hands with moonlight
in a silver bowl
has to be exclusive.
Therefore someone must be banned.
Who? Who? Tell us Pythagoras.
The Thracians yes the Thracians.

But there are no Thracians among us.
We look left and right wondering
who of us could be a secret Thracian
wondering
who of us would say
with the voice of insurrection
I love you
I love you
not in a bullet proof room
and not with his eyes closed.

Pythagoras also maintains
that Thracians have blue hair and red eyes.
Now all day we loiter near the gates
hoping to encounter someone of this description
so that what is now a Religion
can triumphantly become a Society.

3 The summer conference

On grassy lawns
modern black-garbed priests
and scientists in long white coats
confer and dally.

Soon the superintendent will begin
his arcane disquisition
on the new bizarre secret weapon.
(Pssst – the earwigs of R.A.F. Odiham)
Meanwhile I – surprise surprise –
observe something rather remarkable
over there.

Nobody else sees it (near the thornbush)
the coffin rising out of the ground
the old smelly magician himself no less
rising out of the coffin.

He gathers about him his mothy purple cloak.

Daft and drunk with spells
he smiles lopsidedly.
His feet munch on gravel.

He is coming he is coming here
(Hi brighteyes! Hiya brighteyes!)
he is waving that unconvincing
wand he bought in Woolworths.
He has dipped it in a luminous
low-grade oil pool.
Bored with his own act he shouts
JEHOVAH ONE BAAL NIL
Then a lightning flash ha ha
a bit of a rumble of thunder.
Nothing much you understand.
Why should the aged peacock
stretch his wings?

At once the scientists take off
the priests hurry up
into the sky. They zoom.
They free-wheel high over rooftops
playing guitars;
they perform exquisite
figures of 8
but the old mediocre reprobate
merely shrinks them
then returns to his smelly coffin.
Slowly winking he pulls down the lid
slowly the coffin sinks into the ground.
(Bye brighteyes! Arrivederci brighteyes!)

I wave. I blink.
The thunder has cleared
the summer afternoon is vacated.
As if a cannon had been fired
doves and crows
circle the abandoned green lawns.

4 The poetry reading

Coughing and echo of echoes.
A lofty resonant public place.
It is the assembly hall.
Wooden chairs on wooden planks.
Suddenly he enters suddenly
a hush but for the small
distraction of one chair
squeaking in torment on a plank
then his voice unnatural.

He is an underground vatic poet.
His purple plastic coat is enchanting.
Indeed he is chanting
'Fu-er-uck Fu-er-uck'
with spiritual concentration.
Most of us laugh
because the others are laughing
most of us clap
because the others are clapping.

In the Interval out of focus
in the foyer Mr Poet signs his books.
My atheist uncle asseverates
that opus you read Fuck Fuck –
a most affecting and effective
social protest Mr Poet.

In the ladies' corner though
Marian eyeing the bard
maintains he is a real
sexual messiah
that his poem was not an expletive
but an incitement.
Fat Blondie cannot cease from crying.
She thinks his poem so nostalgic.

Meanwhile the superintendent asks
Mr Poet what is a poem?
The first words Eve spoke to Adam?
The last words Adam spoke to Eve
as they slouched from Paradise?

Mr Poet trembles
he whistles
he shakes his head Oi Oi.
As if his legs were under water
he lifts up and down in slow motion
up and down his heavy feet
he rubs the blood vessels in his eyes
he punches with a steady rhythm
his forehead
and then at last
there is the sound of gritty clockwork
the sound of a great whirring.

He is trying to say something.
His sputum is ostentatious
his voice comes through the long ago.

After the interval
the hall clatters raggedly into silence.
Somewhere else distant
a great black bell is beating
the sound of despair
and then is still.
Cu-er-unt Cu-er-unt chants the poet.
We applaud politely
wonder whether he is telling or asking.
The poet retires a trifle ill.
We can all see that he requires air.

5 Visiting day

The superintendent told us
that last summer on vacation
he saw a blind poet
reading Homer
on a Greek mountainside.

As a result my atheist uncle
has fitted black lenses
into his spectacles.
They are so opaque
he cannot see through them.
He walks around with a white stick.
We shout Copycat Copycat.

In reply his mouth utters
I don't want to see I can't bear to see
any more junk dropping down.
Meanwhile visitors of different sizes
in circumspect clothes in small groups
are departing from the great lawns –
though one alone lags behind and is waving.

She in that blue orgone dress waving
reminds me how I wrote a letter once.
'Love read this though it has little meaning
for by reading this you give me meaning'
I wrote or think I wrote or meant to write
and receiving no reply I heard
the silence.
Now I see a stranger waving.

October evenings are so moody.
A light has gone on
in the superintendent's office.
There are rumours that next week
all of us will be issued
with black specs.

Maybe yes maybe no.

But now the gates have closed
now under the huge unleafy trees
there is nobody.
Father father there is no-one.
We are only middle-aged.
There are too many ghosts already.
We remain behind like evergreens.

6 Autumn in Funland

These blue autumn days
we turn on the water taps.
Morse knockings in the pipes
dark pythagorean
interpretations.

The more we know
the more we journey into ignorance.

All day mysterious aeroplanes
fly over
leaving theurgic vapour trails
dishevelled by the wind
horizontal chalky lines
from some secret script
announcing names perhaps
of those about to die.

Downstairs the superintendent
sullen as a ruined millionaire
says nothing does nothing
stares through the dust-flecked window.
He will not dress a wound even.
He cannot stop a child from crying.

Again at night
shafting through the dark
on the bedroom walls
a veneer wash of radium
remarkably disguised
as simple moonlight.
My vertebral column
is turning into glass.

O remember
the atrocities of the Thracians.
They are deadly cunning.
Our water is polluted.
Our air is polluted.
Soon our orifices will bleed.

These black revolving nights
we are all funambulists.
The stars below us
the cerebellum disordered
we juggle on the edge of the earth
one foot on earth
one foot over the abyss.

7 Death of a superintendent

With considerable poise
in a darkening room
the superintendent sat immobile
for hours at the polished table.
His heart had stopped in the silence
between two beats.

Down with the Thracians.
Down with the Thracians
who think God has blue hair and red eyes.
Down with the bastard Thracians
who somehow killed our superintendent.

Yesterday the morning of the funeral
as instructed by Pythagoras
all members on waking kept their eyes closed
all stared at the blackness
in the back of their eyelids
all heard far away five ancient sounds fading.

Today it's very cold.
Fat Blondie stands inconsolable
in the middle of the goldfish pool.
She will not budge.
The musky waters have amputated her feet.
Both her eyes are crying simultaneously.
She holds her shoes in her right hand
and cries and cries.

Meantime our American guest tries
the sophistry of a song.
The only happiness we know she sings
is the happiness that's gone
and Mr Poet moans like a cello
that's most itself when most melancholy.

To all of this
my atheist uncle responds magnificently.
In his funeral black specs
he will be our new leader.
Look how spitting on his hands first
he climbs the flagpole.
Wild at the very top he shouts
I AM IMMORTAL.

8 Lots of snow

First the skies losing height
then snow raging and the revolution bungled.
Afterwards in the silence
between two snowfalls
we deferred to our leader.
We are but shrubs not tall cedars.

Let Pythagoras be
an example to all Thracian spies
my tyrant uncle cried
retiring to the blackness inside
a fat Edwardian pillar box.

Who's next for the icepick?

Already the severed head of Pythagoras
transforms the flagpole
into a singularly
long white neck.

It has become a god that cannot see
how the sun drips its dilutions
on dumpy snowacres.

And I? I write a letter to someone nameless
in white ink on white paper
to an address unknown.
Oh love I write
surely love was no less
because less uttered or more accepted?

My bowels are made of glass.
The western skies try to rouge the snow.
I goosestep across this junk of heaven
to post my blank envelope.

Slowly night begins in the corner
where two walls meet.
The cold is on the crocus.
Snows mush and melt
and small lights fall from twigs.

Bright argus-eyed the thornbush.

Approaching the pillar box
I hear its slit of darkness screaming.

9 The end of Funland

Uncle stood behind me
when I read Mr Poet's poster
on the billiard cloth
of the noticeboard:
COME TO THE THORNBUSH TONIGHT
HEAR THE VOICES ENTANGLED IN IT
MERLIN'S
MESMER'S
ALL THE UNSTABLE MAGICIANS
YEH YEH
DR BOMBASTUS TOO
FULL SUPPORTING CAST.

Not me I said thank you no
I'm a rational man touch wood.
Mesmer is dead these many years
and his purple cloak in rags.

They are all dead replied uncle
don't you know yet
                    all of them dead –
gone where they don't play billiards
haven't you heard the news?

And Elijah the meths drinker
what about Elijah I asked
who used to lie on a parkbench
in bearded sleep – he too?

Of course sneered uncle
smashed smashed years ago like the rest of them
gone with the ravens gone with the lightning.
Why else each springtime
with the opening of a door
no-one's there?

Now at the midnight ritual
we invoke Elijah Merlin Mesmer the best of them
gone with the ravens gone with the lightning
as we stand as usual in concentric circles
around the thornbush.
Something will happen tonight.

Next to me fat Blondie sobs.
Latterly she is much given to sobbing.
The more she sobs the more she suffers.

Suddenly above us
frightful insane
the full moon breaks free from a cloud
stares both ways
and the stars in their stalls tremble.

It enters the black arena aghast
at being seen and by what it can see.
It hoses cold fire over the crowd
over the snowacres of descending
unending slopes.

At last in the distance we hear
the transmigration of souls
like clarinets untranquil played by ghosts
that some fools think to be the wind.

Fat Blondie stops her crying
tilts her face towards me amazed
and holds my hand as if I too were dying.
For a moment I feel as clean as snow.

Do not be misled I say
sometimes Funland can be beautiful
But she takes her hand away.

I can see right through her.
She has become luminous glass.
She is dreaming of the abyss.
We are all dreaming of the abyss
when we forget what we are dreaming of.

But now this so-called moonlight
is changing us all to glass.
We must disperse say goodbye.
We cannot see each other.
Goodbye Blondie goodbye uncle goodbye.

Footsteps in the snow
resume slowly up the slope.

They gave me chewing gum so I chewed.

Who's next for the icepick?

Tell me are we ice or are we glass?

Ask Abaris who stroked my gold thigh.

Fu-er-uck fu-er-uck.

Do not wake us. We may die.

Ghosts, angels, unicorns

I

Thick curtains closed on a knee-knocking table.
That tall androgynous one, half entranced,
who speaks in an ersatz voice, surely knows
that off-duty ghosts prefer daylight?

Once the ghost of Goethe spoke for them all:
'More light!' Ghosts are the colour of air. They like
lamp-posts that blaze in the streets of morning.
They grin in sunbeams where their small dust shows.

But at night they are hellishly employed
by us: have no leisure to haunt olde inns,
to peacock-screech in Highgate Cemetery
or rap tables. We rarely cease from dreaming.

We moan in sleep and they rush from the wings.
We summon through trap doors a non-union cast.
Weeping they scurry from dream to dream.
We produce them, give them impossible scripts.

2

Most are innocent, shy, will not undress.
They own neither genitals nor pubic hair.
Only the fallen of the hierarchy
make an appearance these secular days.

No longer useful as artists' models,
dismissed by theologians, morale tends
to be low – even high-class angels grumble
as they loiter in our empty churches.

Neutered, they hide when a gothic door opens.
Sudden light blinds them, footsteps deafen,
Welsh hymns stampede their shadows entirely.
Still their stink lingers, cold stone and incense.

But the fallen dare even 10 Downing Street,
astonish, fly through walls for their next trick;
spotlit, enter the dreams of the important,
slowly open their gorgeous Carnaby wings.

3

Were they the first of things to disappear
or just mistranslations from the Hebrew?
Invisible, they graze near stone bridges over streams.
When they drink, sunlight shakes beneath an arch.

They love the forlorn convolvulus flower
of Scotland in which they scratch their flaccid horn.
With eyes closed they think we don't exist.
The gift of sanity no longer theirs.

Their fabulous hoofs make little noise.
They breathe no air and feed upon the dark
no louder than insects that strike the fast
windscreens of cars travelling through summer nights.

Past dawn when there's no more dark to eat
their white horn grows, seeks out a maiden.
Mounted, Sleeping Beauty sighs and stirs,
the gift of sanity no longer hers.

Watching a cloud

A lacy mobile changing lazily
its animals, unstable faces, till
I imagine an angel, his vapours sailing
asleep at different speeds. My failing:

to see similes, cloud as something other.
Is all inspiration correspondences?
Machinery of cloud and angel both are silent,
both insubstantial. Neither violent.

And, truly, if one shining angel existed
what safer than the camouflage of a cloud?
There's deranged wind up there. God its power!
Let me believe in angels for an hour.

Let sunlight fade on walls and a huge blind
be drawn faster than a horse across this field.
I want to be theological, stare through
raw white angel-fabric at holy bits of blue.

Let long theatrical beams slant down
to stage-strike that hill into religion. Me too!
An angel drifts to the East, its edges burning;
sunny sunlight on stony stone returning.

Three cars

On the cleared site between tall buildings
three cars, inert, point the same way.
Sunlight clings to their edges, falls off.
If monsters, they seem leucotomized,
do not hear the scattered rhythm of workmen
clanging dull metal nearby – nor beyond,
the obscure grumbling of the background.
Their eyes empty. No flies hover.

Through the afternoon they have waited,
rooftop after rooftop obediently.
Now the last sunlight catches, ignites
excitements of fire and sacrifice.
Two, tumescent, thrill with a deep thrumming.
One chokes. They call each to each. They smash
puffs of blue poison from exhaust pipes.
Such joy – brakes released. They are possessed.

And go wild once past the modest suburbs.
They flee: music crackles, dials glow.
Their six eyes light the country dark.
Half dreaming they descend between black woods
until their red tail lamps disappear.
Out of sight they snarl, overtake each other,
dare not mate. They deposit on the roads
just a little oil in the moonlight.

The weeping

After I lean from my shadow
to switch on the dark in the lamp,
I sense distant riders
and a disembodied crone-voice rasping,
'Do not weep like a woman
for what you would not fight for as a man.'
Eyes closed before sleep
I think how sleep is a going into exile;
how shadows also
are but cut-out pieces of darkness
exiled from darkness.
(Each summer's day especially,
the diaspora of shadows
awaits the return of night.)

Already, clearly, I hear the advance
of horses, their regular pounding.
Soon two shadows on horseback appear:
one Boabdil, a king long dead,
the other, his scolding mother.
What is dream, what is not dream?
They ride round the corner
of night. They loom near
and become substance. They halt
their horses. They look back
at the alhambra of fable.
(Years since I, a tourist, sauntered
in the alhambra of fable,
read their guidebook story.)

Not the most woeful sound a man may hear,
an exile weeping and weeping.
Yet desolate it is
like a ram's horn blown
in a hushed synagogue,
like Christian bells opening, closing,
like the muezzin heard
even after he has ceased.
Such is the sound this man makes
looking back with clarifying remorse.
No man weeping either,
but a silhouette of a man,
a hunched shadow on horseback,
a homeless shadow weeping.

And I wake up
weeping. I and another both weep
in the darkness, weep in unison.
I wake up. I sit up and stop weeping.
No-one weeps.

Florida

Not one poem about an animal, she said,
in five, six volumes of poetry,
not one about The Peaceable Kingdom.
An accusation. Was she from the RSPCA?
Your contemporaries have all composed
inspired elegies for expired beasts;
told of salmon flinging themselves up
the sheer waterfall; cold crows,
in black rags, loitering near motorways;
parables of foxes and pheasants,
owls and voles, mice and moles,
cats, bats, pigs, pugs, snails, quails;
so why can't you write one, just one *haiku*?
Oh, I said, Oh! – then wondered if she knew
the story of the starving dowager.

The lady looked as solemn as No.
Well, during the French Revolution,
the dowager, becoming thinner and thinner,
invited other lean aristocrats to dinner.
That night the guests saw (I continued)
slowly roasting on a rotating spit
the dowager's own poodle, Fido,
who proved to be most succulent.
So they made a feast of it.
Afterwards, the dowager sighed,
fingering the pearls about her neck,
sighed and said in noble French,
(I translate) What a damn shame Fido
isn't alive to eat up all those nice
crunchy bones left upon the plate.

My story over, I waited for applause. We'd
never cease from crying, she said,
if *one* insect could relate its misery.
Quite, I said, looking at my paws.
In Florida I saw a floating log
change and chase and swallow up
a barking dog. Hell, I said, an alligator?
A museum snake, too, in Gainesville,
Murder City, I can't forget,
poor black priapus in an empty case
lifting up its head for food not there.
With your gift I'd make a poem out of that.
So try, she said, do try and write
a creature poem and call it *Florida*.
I closed my eyes and she receded.

I thought of tigers and of Blake,
I thought of Fido and his bones.
No, no, she cried, think of Florida.
I saw the hotels of Miami Beach,
I heard waves collapsing ceaselessly.
No no, she said, think again, think
of Florida, its creature kingdom.
Like a TV screen my imagination
lit up to startle the ghost of Blake
with my own eidetic ads for Florida:
first, that black frustrated snake erect,
then two grapefruit inside a brassière.
Open your eyes, the lady screamed, *wake up*.
I'm a poor bifurcated animal, I apologized.
Eagle beagle, bug grub, boar bear.

The silence of Tudor Evans

Gwen Evans, singer and trainer of singers,
who, in 1941, warbled
an encore (Trees) at Porthcawl Pavilion
lay in bed, not half her weight and dying.
Her husband, Tudor, drew the noise of curtains.

Then, in the artificial dark, she whispered,
'Please send for Professor Mandlebaum.'
She raised her head pleadingly from the pillow,
her horror-movie eyes thyrotoxic.
'Who?' Tudor asked, remembering, remembering.

Not Mandlebaum, not that renowned professor
whom Gwen had once met on holiday;
not that lithe ex-Wimbledon tennis player
and author of *Mediastinal Tumours*;
not that swine Mandlebaum of 1941?

Mandlebaum doodled in his hotel bedroom.
For years he had been in speechless sloth.
But now for Gwen and old times' sake he, first-class,
alert, left echoing Paddington for
a darkened sickroom and two large searching eyes.

She sobbed when he gently took her hand in his.
'But, my dear, why are you crying?'
'Because, Max, you're quite unrecognizable.'
'I can't scold you for crying about that,'
said Mandlebaum and he, too, began to weep.

They wept together (and Tudor closed his eyes)
        Gwen, singer and trainer of singers,
because she was dying; and he, Mandlebaum,
        ex-physician and ex-tennis player,
because he had become so ugly and so old.

Uncle Isidore

When I observe a toothless ex-violinist,
with more hair than face, sprawled like Karl Marx
on a park seat or slumped, dead or asleep,
in the central heat of a public library
I think of Uncle Isidore – smelly
schnorrer and lemon-tea bolshevik – my foreign
distant relative, not always distant.

Before Auschwitz, Treblinka, he seemed near,
those days of local pogroms, five year programmes,
until I heard him say, 'Master, Master
of the Universe, blessed be your name,
don't you know there's been no rain for years
and your people are thirsty? Have you no shame,
compassion? Don't you care at all?'

And fitting the violin to his beard
he bitterly asked me – no philosopher
but a mere boy – 'What difference between
the silence of God and the silence of men?'
Then, distant, as if in the land of Uz,
the answering sky let fall the beautiful
evening sound of thunder and of serious rain.

That was the first time Uncle went lame,
the first time the doctor came and quit hopelessly.
His right foot raised oddly to his left knee,
some notes wrong, all notes wild, unbalanced,
he played and he played not to that small child
who, big-eyed, listened – but to the Master
of the Universe, blessed be his name.

Tales of Shatz

Meet Rabbi Shatz in his correct black homburg.
The cheder boys call him Ginger.
If taller than 5 foot you're taller than he;
also taller than his father,
grandfather, great grandfather.

Meet Ruth Shatz, née Ruth Pinsky,
short-statured too, straight-backed.
In her stockinged feet
her forehead against his,
her eyes smile into his.
And again on the pillow, later.
Ah those sexy red-headed Pinskys
of Leeds and Warsaw: her mother,
grandmother, great grandmother!

Mrs Shatz resembles Rabbi Shatz's mother.
Rabbi Shatz resembles Mrs Shatz's father.
Strangers mistake them for brother, sister.

At University, Solly Shatz, their morning star,
suddenly secular, all 6 foot of him –
a black-haired centre-forward on Saturdays –
switches studies from Theology to Genetics.

*

A certain matron of Golders Green,
fingering amber beads about her neck,
approaches Rabbi Shatz.
When I was a small child, she thrills,
once, just once, God the Holy One
came through the curtains of my bedroom.
What on earth has he been doing since?

Rabbi Shatz turns, he squints,
he stands on one leg
hoping for the inspiration of a Hillel.
The Holy One, he answers, blessed be He,
has been waiting, waiting patiently,
till you see Him again.

★

Consider the mazzle of Baruch Levy
who changed his name to Barry Lee,
who moved to Esher, Surrey,
who sent his four sons – Matthew, Mark,
Luke and John – to boarding school,
who had his wife's nose fixed,
who, blinking in the Gents,
turned from the writing on the wall
and later, still blinking, joined the golf club.

With new friend, Colonel Owen,
first game out, under vexed clouds,
thunder detonated without rain,
lightning stretched without thunder,
and near the 2nd hole,
where the darker green edged
to the shaved lighter green,
both looked up terrified.
Barbed fire zagged towards them
to strike dead instantly
Mostyn Owen, Barry Lee's opponent.
What luck that Colonel Owen
(as Barry discovered later)
once was known as Moshe Cohen.

Now, continued Rabbi Shatz,
recall how even the sorrows of Job
had a happy ending.

*

Being a religious man Shatz adored riddles.
Who? he asked his impatient wife.

Who like all men came into this world
with little fists closed, departed
with large hands open, yet on walking
over snow and away from sunsets
followed no shadow in front of him,
left no footprint behind him?

You don't know either, opined his wife.
You and your Who? Who?
Are you an owl?
Why do you always pester me with riddles
you don't know the answer of?

Rabbi Shatz for some reason wanted to cry.
If I knew the answers, he whispered,
would my questions still be riddles?
And he tiptoed away, closed the door
so softly behind him
as if on a sleeping dormitory.

Often when listening to music
before a beautiful slow movement
recaptured him, Shatz would blank out,
hear nothing. So now, too, in his lit study
as night rain tilted outside
across dustbins in the lane
he forgot why his lips moved, his body swayed.

Cousin Sidney

Dull as a bat, said my mother
of cousin Sidney in 1940 that time he tried
to break his garden swing, jumping on it,
size 12 shoes – at fifteen the tallest boy
in the class, taller than loping Dan Morgan
when Dan Morgan wore his father's top hat.

Duller than a bat, said my father
when hero Sidney lied about his age
to claim rough khaki, silly ass;
and soon, somewhere near Dunkirk,
some foreign corner was forever Sidney
though uncle would not believe it.

Missing not dead please God, please,
he said, and never bolted the front door,
never string taken from the letter box,
never the hall light off lest his one son
came home through a night of sleet
whistling, We'll meet again.

Aunt crying and raw in the onion air
of the garden (the unswinging empty swing)
her words on a stretched leash
while uncle shouted, Bloody Germans.
And on November 11th, two howls
of silence even after three decades

till last year, their last year,
when uncle and aunt also went missing,
missing alas, so that now strangers
have bolted their door and cut the string
and no-one at all (the hall so dark)
waits up for Sidney, silly ass.

Remembrance Day

Unbuttoned at home, last Sunday afternoon,
Violence snored in the armchair.
This week, eyes moist, our neighbour marches
with the veterans, ready to be televised,
his nationalism narrow as the coffin
in which the invented hero lies.

A vision dies from being too long stared at.
Not only songs of the old wars fade but ghosts
on barbed wire, on a bayonet-blade. Yet still
everything is what it is and another thing
as the black-coated ceremonies begin
under a vapour trail in blue cold skies.

2000 men are taking off their hats. Not one cries
'Folly'; not one from somewhere else
when the hollow trumpets toot and the guns
damply thud. Echo of an echo of an echo
vanishing like that vapour trail.
Whatever happened to you, Dolly?

By nightfall, smoke lurks down pub-lit streets
and cheers! cheers! mademoiselle from 'Armentiers';
and did you die of cancer, Lily Marlene?
You have forgotten, cannot touch the pinewood.
So Violence, beery, lonely as an old tune,
lifts his lapel to smell the paper poppy.

The test

From a park bench I stare at Centre Point
and dream of Nell, that witty Protestant whore,
while mild clerks and secretaries carnival the grass
and feed the bolder pigeons. They would not ignore
a king's mistress as they now do this derelict
who tries a little dance, solicits me, alas.

Advances, bows, and becomes eerie, becomes a shade
in sunlight. Yes, it's you, old ghost! You lift
your dress and I see nothing. A bottle gleams
in your right hand, an orange balloon in your left.
Oh the irreducible strangeness of things
and the random purposes of dreams.

You thrust your face into mine. What breweries
of oaths! Then you offer another your mouth to kiss
and ask brashly, 'How's your sex-life, lover?'
I know you haunt lunchtime London for more than this
for now you turn your methylated eyes
to Charles II, the statue with a hangover.

Stoned in Soho Square under high trees!
Soon on clacking typewriters secretaries will rout
the day and I shall worry verses such as these,
if not these. And, suddenly, all is inside out:
the king, quelled, has his back to the stews of Soho
and Nell sinks to the grass on arthritic knees,

seems in hell, weeps on all fours, howls at pigeons,
each second becomes less Nell and more a female Caliban.
Oh no ghost she, but suffering flesh, human and unchaste,
and I, fastidious as any office man,
though licensed friend to Caliban, turn away,
turn from her stridency in slow sorrow and distaste.

Nothing

Amnesia. A keyhole. A glass eye.
In sleep, dreams between long blanks;
awake, blanks between brief dreams.
This is the cemetery side of 50.
This is the taste of pure water.
This is the dread revealing nothing.

Beyond the carpeted staircase
the captive evening settles
where the bedroom door is shut
above a bar of brilliance
that becomes, as the landing darkens
darkens, brighter brighter.

The stethoscope

Through it,
over young women's tense abdomens,
I have heard the sound of creation
and, in a dead man's chest, the silence
before creation began.

Should I
pray therefore? Hold this instrument in awe
and aloft a procession of banners?
Hang this thing in the interior
of a cold, mushroom-dark church?

Should I
kneel before it, chant an apophthegm
from a small text? Mimic priest or rabbi,
the swaying noises of religious men?
Never! Yet I could praise it.

I should
by doing so celebrate my own ears,
by praising them praise speech at midnight
when men become philosophers;
laughter of the sane and insane;

night cries
of injured creatures, wide-eyed or blind;
moonlight sonatas on a needle;
lovers with doves in their throats; the wind
travelling from where it began.

Joan's

Now that the evening cold is on the crocus
do you feel the ache of something missing?
Snow melts falling, a million small lights fuse

on twigs, fall to pools of darkness on the ground
while, indoors, one note's gone from the piano
– the highest. Listen to the thud of felt.

No, dear, no! Hear rather the other notes
of the right hand. Also the left background.
Their rejoicing, lamenting, candid sound.

Smile please

(*For Stuart Evans*)

Young, I'd startle on a dust-free hole in the air,
with electronic or magnesium flash
photograph the other side, reveal reluctant
ghosts or some rare frightful metamorphosis.

I'd catch Leda naked, her face flushed,
her body white like the swan's; or wrathful
Apollo erect and frustrated as Daphne
became less woman, more tree. There were nights

I dreamed a great light picked out momentarily
a unicorn tupping an over-exposed virgin
while other beasts, unknown to man, silently
paced from one secret world to another.

Now the invisible is dark in the blaze of noon
and I'm here and glad beneath a spired church
where over-dressed relatives throw confetti, laugh
and lurch towards a couple enlarged with love.

Older, it's scenes like this that charm me – the
 disguise
of comedy, blossom of a nettle, a wedding
 photograph!
And tonight I'll show you the touched-up proof
as new-minted Mr and Mrs kiss and kiss

to prove no developed metamorphosis
can be so wild or as genuine as this.

Bedtime story

Adam, the first man, my father said, perfect
like the letter A. Blessed be all alephs.
Then my clever question: were there no creatures,

father, before Adam? A long index finger
vertical as a flame to horizontal lips.
Eyes right, eyes left. Whisper of a spy:

yes, unfortunate creatures, angels botched,
badly made, born to be vagrant, born with
the usual amnesia but with little sense

and no sense of direction. They could not
deliver the simplest of messages. . . .
Now, late, I think of that flawed lineage:

of one announcing great news to the wrong Mary
– perhaps it was that unshaved derelict
at the bus station with an empty bottle, muttering –

and here's another in disguise, down at heel,
defeated face white as the salt of Sodom,
veteran among the homeward football crowd

shuffling under hoardings towards nightfall;
and this one supine, over-bearded,
sleeping on a parkbench in his excrement.

Dogs bark and bark at them. They lack pleasure.
They refrigerate the coldness of things.
They stale. They taste the age of their own mouths.

In Casualty rarely cry or grumble.
In wards die with only screens around them.
But now, father, here's *my* bedtime story:

sometimes in the last light of January,
in treeless districts of cities, in a withered
backstreet, their leader can be glimpsed from trains.

He stands motionless in long black overcoat
on spoilt snow and seems like a man again
who yet, father, will outlast the letter Z.

In the gallery

I

Outside it is snow snow
but here, under the chandelier,
there's no such thing as weather.
Right wall, a horse (not by Géricault);
left, a still life, mainly apples;
between, on the parquet floor, a box
or a coffin which is being opened.

Through a gold-framed mirror
the Director, dressed as if for mourning,
observes the bust
of an unknown lady
by an unknown sculptor
being lifted out of the straw
by a man in overalls.

2

The apples do not rot, the horse will not bolt,
the statue of the lady
cannot breathe one spot
of tissue paper on the mirror.

Her name is forgotten,
the sculptor's name is disputed,
they both have disappeared forever.
They could have been born
in the North or the South.
They have no grave anywhere.

3

Outside it is snow snow
snowing and namelessness is growing.

Yesterday four hoofmarks in the snows
rose and flew away.

They must have been four crows.
Or, maybe, three of them were crows.

A winter visit

Now she's ninety I walk through the local park
where, too cold, the usual peacocks do not screech
and neighbouring lights come on before it's dark.

Dare I affirm to her, so agèd and so frail,
that from one pale dot of peacock's sperm
spring forth all the colours of a peacock's tail?

I do. But she like the sibyl says, 'I would die';
then complains, 'This winter I'm half dead, son.'
And because it's true I want to cry.

Yet must not (although only Nothing keeps)
for I inhabit a white coat not a black
even here – and am not qualified to weep.

So I speak of small approximate things,
of how I saw, in the park, four flamingoes
standing, one-legged on ice, heads beneath wings.

The doctor

Guilty, he does not always like his patients.
But here, black fur raised, their yellow-eyed dog
mimics Cerberus, barks barks at the invisible,
so this man's politics, how he may crawl
to superiors, do not matter. A doctor must care
and the wife's on her knees in useless prayer,
the young daughter's like a waterfall.

Quiet, Cerberus! Soon enough you'll have a bone
or two. Now, coughing, the patient expects
the unjudged lie: 'Your symptoms are familiar
and benign' – someone to be cheerfully sure,
to transform tremblings, gigantic unease,
by naming like a pet some small disease
with a known aetiology, certain cure.

So the doctor will and yes he will prescribe
the usual dew from a banana leaf; poppies and
honey too; ten snowflakes or something whiter
from the bole of a tree; the clearest water
ever, melting ice from a mountain lake;
sunlight from waterfall's edge, rainbow smoke;
tears from eyelashes of the daughter.

X-ray

Some prowl sea-beds, some hurtle to a star
and, mother, some obsessed turn over every stone
or open graves to let that starlight in.
There are men who would open anything.

Harvey, the circulation of the blood,
and Freud, the circulation of our dreams,
pried honourably and honoured are
like all explorers. Men who'd open men.

And those others, mother, with diseases
like great streets named after them: Addison,
Parkinson, Hodgkin – physicians who'd arrive
fast and first on any sour death-bed scene.

I am their slowcoach colleague, half afraid,
incurious. As a boy it was so: you know how
my small hand never teased to pieces
an alarm clock or flensed a perished mouse.

And this larger hand's the same. It stretches now
out from a white sleeve to hold up, mother,
your X-ray to the glowing screen. My eyes look
but don't want to; I still don't want to know.

Lunch with a pathologist

My colleague knows by heart the morbid verse
of facts – the dead weight of a man's liver,
a woman's lungs, a baby's kidneys.

At lunch he recited unforgettably,
'After death, of all soft tissues the brain's
the first to vanish, the uterus the last.'

'Yes,' I said, 'at dawn I've seen silhouettes
hunched in a field against the skyline, each one
feasting, preoccupied, silent as gas.

Partial to women they've stripped women bare
and left behind only the taboo food,
the uterus, inside the skeleton.'

My colleague wiped his mouth with a napkin,
hummed, picked shredded meat from his canines,
said, 'You're a peculiar fellow, Abse.'

No reply

Why?
                                        because
when I went home no one was home
because I knew I was awake
(a man asleep is a man enslaved)
I stood up walked into the hall
where I dialled the number
because of some strange ancestor
because I'm Welsh because I'm a Jew
because the audible clock's rounder
than any circle I can draw
because I've shared the particular
lunatic boredom of caged animals
because I've been touched on a scar
and felt nothing or almost nothing
because when sick I'm still a doctor
because pathologists aver
'The first organ to disappear

is the brain – the uterus the last'
because I shan't forget that ever
because I walked into the hall where
I stood next to the telephone
I thought of a number doubled it.

Orpheus in the surgery

They say the accompanying god,
when you turned abruptly to your wife,
held her fast and cried resigned, 'He has turned!'
But she, grasping nothing, whispered, '*Who?*'
How often, lost at some terminal bed,
have I recalled her question, been moved by it.

Doctor, you're fooled, that story's half untrue.
When I raised high the torch and slowly turned

I saw no one and no one spoke but me.
I dare say, far below, Ixion's wheel stopped,

sweating Sisyphus paused, shoulder to the rock,
and the forty-nine daughters of Danaus

stood still, their profiles listening. For they knew,
being accursed, my secret – why I had turned.

But above, at the eye-creasing O, the crowds,
those living silhouettes awaiting me

under the active bunting, the dignitaries,
TV crews, they did not know and asked, 'Why?'

So I lied – call it poet's gossip – not daring
to confess, as I now do, my absurd,

obscene imaginings: how I'd thought a stranger –
no god he – had sexually sipped my wife;

how she, in turn, all glue, moaned such vile
endearments, such drowsy syrups of love.

That's why I raised the torch, why in anguish,
doctor, it was I, not she, who whispered, '*Who?*'

Pantomime diseases

When the fat Prince french-kissed Sleeping Beauty
her eyelids opened wide. She heard applause,
the photographer's shout, wedding-guest laughter.
Poor girl – she married the Prince out of duty
and suffered insomnia ever after.

The lies of Once-upon-a-Time appal.
Cinderella seeing white mice grow into horses
shrank to the wall – an event so ominous
she didn't go to the Armed Forces Ball
but phoned up Alcoholics Anonymous.

Snow White suffered from profound anaemia.
The genie warned, 'Aladdin, you'll go blind,'
when that little lad gleefully rubbed his lamp.
The Babes in the Wood died of pneumonia.
D. Whittington turned back because of cramp.

Shy, in the surgery, Red Riding Hood undressed
– Dr Wolff, the fool, diagnosed Scarlet Fever.
That Jill who tumbled down has wrecked her back,
that Puss-in-Boots has gout and is depressed
and one bare bear gave Goldilocks a heart attack.

When the three Darling children thought they'd fly
to Never-Never Land – the usual trip –
their pinpoint pupils betrayed addiction.
And not hooked by Captain Hook but by
that ponce, Peter Pan! All the rest is fiction.

Of Rabbi Yose

I know little except he would ponder
on the meaning of words in the Torah
till those words became more mysterious
became an astonishment and an error.

'Thou shalt grope at noonday
as the blind gropeth in darkness.'
Soon Yose's eyebrows raised
from that poetry page of curses.
Instead he stared at the adventure
of a white wall and said, 'What difference
to a blind man, noon or midnight?'

All that week, all that month
he puzzled it, '. . . as the blind gropeth . . .',
not reading it as a child would
without obstruction, nor understanding it
as a child could. He thought, too,
of his neighbour, the blind man.

Then coming home late one night
after discussing the Torah with a pupil,
or sickness with a sick man,
one suffering perhaps from the botch
of Egypt, or from emerods, or the scab,

he saw near the darkest foliage
the plumed yellow flame of a torch
moving towards him, held high in the hand
of his neighbour, the blind man.

'Neighbour,' he cried, 'why this torch
since you are blind?' The night waited
for an answer: the wind in a carob tree,
two men, one blind, both bearded, so many
shadows thrown and fleeing from the torch.

'So that others may see me, of course,'
replied the neighbour, 'and save me
from quicksand and rock, from the snake asleep,
from cactus, from thistle and from thornbush,
from the deep potholes in the roadway.'

Year after year, to pupil after pupil,
Yose told of this night-meeting,
told it as parable, told it smiling,
satisfied, with clear-seeing eyes,
and never again pondered the true
lucid meaning of the words:
'Thou shalt grope at noonday
as the blind gropeth in darkness.'

Snake

When the snake bit
Rabbi Hanina ben Dosa
while he was praying

the snake died. (Each day
is attended by surprises
or it is nothing.)

Question: was the bare-footed,
smelly Rabbi more poisonous
than the snake

or so God-adulterated
he'd become immune
to serpent poison?

Oh great-great-great-uncles,
your palms weighing air,
why are you arguing?

Listen, the snake thought
(being old and unwell
and bad-tempered as hell)

Death, where's thy sting?
In short, was just testing:
a snake's last fling.

Yes, the *so-called* snake
was dying anyway, its heart
calcified and as old as Eden.

No, that snake was A1 fit
but while hissing for fun it
clumsily bit its own tongue.

No, Hanina invented that snake;
not for his own sake but for first-
class, religious publicity.

No no, here's the key to it.
Ask: did the Rabbi, later on,
become a jumpy, timid man?

Remember, he who has been bitten
by a snake thereafter becomes
frightened of a rope. . . .

Bearded men in darkening rooms
sipping lemon tea and arguing
about the serpent till the moon

of Russia, of Latvia, Lithuania,
Poland, rose above the alien
steeples – centuries of sleep.

Now, tonight, a clean-shaven rabbi
who once studied in Vienna
says snake-venom contains

haemolysins, haemo-
coagulants, protolysins,
cytolysins and neurotoxins

and that even in Hanina
ben Dosa's day a snake was a
snake – unless, of course, it was

a penis, an unruly penis,
making a noise like one pissing
on a mound of fresh hot ashes.

Oh great-great-great-uncles
did you hear him? And are your
handbones weighing moonshine?

Of Itzig and his dog

To pray for the impossible,
says Itzig, is disgraceful.
I prefer, when I'm on my own,
when I'm only with my dog,
when I can't go out
because of the weather,
because of my shoes,
to talk very intimately to God.

Itzig, they nag, why do that,
what's the point of that?
God never replies surely?

Such ignorance! Am I at the Western Wall?
Am I on spacious Mount Sinai?
Is there a thornbush in this murky room?
God may never say a word,
may never even whisper, Itzig, hullo.

But when I'm talking away
to the right and to the left,
when it's raining outside,
when there's rain on the glass,
when I say please God this
and thank God that,
then God always makes, believe me,
the dog's tail wag.

Jottings I

Seekers after truth

Questing, he climbs and climbs, mad-eyed,
far from the dancer and the lyre;
but when he looks up towards the blue
always the mountain grows higher.

Below, distant, the roaring courtiers
rise to their feet – less shocked than irate.
Salome has dropped the seventh veil
and they've discovered there are eight.

Don Juan reports

In the evening she looked like Rachel sweetly
and sweetly said, 'Make yourself feel at home.'
But in the morning she looked like Leah plainly
and I thought I'd rather feel at home at home.

Inspiration

Above Professor Einstein's bed
a portrait of Isaac Newton.
One night Einstein bit an apple and
that portrait fell upon his head.

Jottings 2

Transgression

When Eve held in her right hand
the forbidden apple
nothing happened.
So she took a little bite,
a cautious little bite,
and nothing happened.
The great sun shone,
the waterfall fell,
the Paradise birds continued to sing,
so she took another bite
and then another bite,
munch munch munch,
until she'd swallowed the whole damned thing.

Song of himself

Whatever was broken, rejected or lost,
he would, thrillingly amok, sing its praises
and for the length of his eye-brimming song
he would feel like some strange, magnificent king,
not one broken, rejected and lost.

Street scene

(*Outside the grocer's, Golders Green Road*)

They quarrel, this black-bearded man
and his busy, almost flying wife –
she with her hands, he with proverbs.

'He who never rebukes his son,'
says the bearded man too blandly,
'leads him into delinquency.'

And she who hasn't studied nicely
such studied wisdom, now replies,
'You're a, you're a, you're a donkey.'

Three or four psychiatrists smile
as they pass the greengrocer's shop.
Again, patient, he quotes the Talmud:

'When one suggests you're a donkey
do not fret; only when two speak thus
go buy yourself a saddle.'

But she has thrown appropriate
carrots carrots at his sober head
and one sticks brightly in his beard.

Truce! You have been led into fiction.
Listen! Here comes a violin
and tunes to make a donkey dance.

The bearded man has closed his eyes.
Who's this, disguised as a beggar,
playing a violin without strings?

What music's this, its cold measure?
Who are these, dangling from lampposts,
kicking as if under water?

The empty building at night

This busy morning the ten-year-old office tower
was still unoccupied, still halfway up
to an aeroplane that pursued Heathrow,
and I went to work, frowned at the enthronement
of emptiness, was not appeased by
its compelling stories of uncurtained windows,
swarming rumours of ghost clouds, ghost sky.

Now, tonight, late, head down, hurrying home
I would ignore the dark building devoid of men
and deny again that the emptiness inside it
is part of my life, loathed by me because so;
yet I do look up, as if by ordinance, to see alas
what I knew I would: the wakeful moon too near,
untenanted, terrific on its glass.

Lights in the night suburb

I

The first perfect night of the New Year
and there is the obvious moon and here
are the lights no one foretold, springing
like oblongs to bedroom windows
across the road from each other.

2

At the third stroke it will be 9.24 p.m.
and Joanna Cash draws her right hand
first to the right and then to the left
to create the shuffling metallic
interrupted sound of pulled curtains.

At 9.25 p.m. bespectacled Isaac Parr,
the neighbour opposite in No. 26,
hands in pockets, approaches the brilliant
bare blackness of *his* bedroom window
and, somewhat lonely, peers out at lampposts.

This is London. Joanna Cash and Isaac Parr
do not know each other, never will.
Soon Isaac Parr will lurk downstairs,
switch on TV. Soon Joanna Cash
will wash her hair with the product
frequently advertised on TV.

3

Surely, earlier, one of the old gods
furtively walked through the night suburbs,
beard tilted forty-five degrees towards the moon,
saw windows light up conspiratorially
and was frightened into vanishings?

For now the street is deserted.
Not a footstep.
Lost under the furthest lamppost
a still round blob of moonlight.
Perfect night, perfect cloudless night.

The power of prayer

A kind of tune, heart in pilgrimage, yes,
   but reversed thunder as Herbert said?
Herbert was right or we were April fools
last night when we beheld a sign. Behold!
   our Indian neighbour surely praying
since every house across the road was dark
except his own – his bedroom lit by volts,
no doubt, of the thunderstruck eternal.
Why else would those high surprising windows
be raging steadily with sheet lightning?

Herbert, such prayer-power! You'd not credit
   these other, raving, more ancient gods
summoned here by fervent invitation.
How they swarmed in rudely, none so rampant
   as Agni – tawny hair, all gold teeth,
long golden beard – whooping it up crazy
in that attic crackling room, his crimson
snorting horses and his dwarf golden car.
These wild, drunken fire deities! Neighbour,
we thought, oh cease praying do, for God's sake.

And just in case called the bell-mad earthly
 fire brigade whose hoses curved and hushed
so that the gods quit, disguised cleverly,
of course, as tiny butterflies of fire
 or billowing out in cloaks of smoke
and sacred steam. Now no more thunderstorms,
only black debris of last night's party.
And so we godless ones give thanks to God
for godless neighbours this April morning
and for ladders more than rainbows, Herbert.

Night village

No hare pulls a legless man screaming
into the headlights by his beard.
Driving through the night is not dreaming.

Now it's after two and we are close
to a village asleep which is no
place much. It seems to be all there is.

Here's a few small shops, their unseen glass.
Here's two great dazzling headlights
approaching selfishly. They do not pass.

For at the far corner they are thrown
nowhere. Opposite the Shell garage
closed, suddenly, they're proved to be our own.

This is the brief empty blazing High Street
connecting the one dark road coming in
to the one dark road going out.

And we accelerate, become the speed
of night. Behind us, silence resumes while,
in the mirror, the village lights recede.

No hare pulls a legless man screaming
into the headlights by his beard.
Driving through the night is not dreaming.

Light

Waking from a poorly lit dream
so fast forgetting it
that coming downstairs whistling
I forgot even forgetting.

A letter said, Poets should hold up
lamps in bad light. Why? That others
may see the corpse with placard round
its neck. I could smell gas.

And this for breakfast. The only
permitted whistling seemed to be
the victim's severed windpipe.
Now morning sky dull as ashes.

Forgive me corpse with placard round
your neck. And you, dybbuk, whistling.
Sometimes a man must close his eyes
and ears. So letter to the waste-basket.

Yet, later, rapping the table
without intent, noise in my knuckles,
I discovered the sudden gleam of dead
light from last night's dream.

Less a discovery than a recovery.
Silence and glass in a room –
glass in the window and glass
in the mirror facing that window.

A note to Donald Davie in Tennessee

Wigged gluttony never your style but will you
always eschew,
barbered, the anorexia of fanaticism?
Though we would seldom sign the same petition
or join awkwardly the same shouting march,
neither of us, I hope, would leave through those doors
on the right or on the left marked HYGIENE.

Donald, you're such a northern-rooted man
you've moved again.
Is home only home away from it? Still poets
jog eagerly, each molehill mistaken
for Parnassus – such energy articulate!
But where's the avant-garde when the procession
runs continuously in a closed circle?

So many open questions to one who prefers
fugitive ways.
Of course I salute your gifted contradictions –
your two profiles almost the same – like Martin
Guerre's.
I too am a reluctant puritan, feel uneasy
sometimes as if I travelled without ticket.
Yet here I am in England way out in the centre.

A sea-shell for Vernon Watkins

A stage moon and you, too, unreal, unearthed.
Then two shadows athletic down the cliffs
of Pennard near the nightshift of the sea.
You spoke of Yeats and Dylan, your sonorous
pin-ups. I thought, *relentless romantic!*
Darkness stayed in a cave and I lifted
a sea-shell from your shadow when you big-talked
how the dead resume the silence of God.

The bank calls in its debts and all are earthed.
Only one shadow at Pennard today
and listening to another sea-shell I found,
startled, its phantom sea utterly silent
– the shell's cochlea scooped out. Yet appropriate
that small void, that interruption of sound,
for what should be heard in a shell at Pennard
but the stopped breath of a poet who once sang loud?

Others gone also, like you dispensable,
famed names once writ in gold on spines of books
now rarely opened, the young asking, 'Who?'
The beaches of the world should be strewn with such
dumb shells while the immortal sea syllables
in self-love its own name, 'Sea, Sea, Sea, Sea.'
I turn to leave Pennard. This shell is useless.
If I could cry I would but not for you.

Imitations

In this house, in this afternoon room,
my son and I. The other side of glass
snowflakes whitewash the shed roof and the grass
this surprised April. My son is sixteen,
an approximate man. He is my chameleon,
my soft diamond, my deciduous evergreen.

Eyes half closed he listens to pop forgeries
of music – how hard it is to know – and perhaps
dreams of some school Juliet I don't know.
Meanwhile, beyond the bending window,
gusting suddenly, despite a sky half blue,
a blur of white blossom, whiter snow.

And I stare, oh immortal springtime, till
I'm elsewhere and the age my cool son is,
my father alive again (I, his duplicate),
his high breath, my low breath, sticking to the glass
while two white butterflies stumble, held each
to each as if by elastic, and pass.

One Sunday afternoon

In the courtyard my son with a football.
Here, a woodwormed room fit for suicide.
Locus suspectus. Oakbeams the hack described
where the squire swung two hundred years ago
to become, according to the guidebook,
transparent. Despite leaves falling outside
who can believe in ghosts? Especially in daylight!

So if something stood now against those curtains
to wear their exact design, and if somehow
the window opened slowly like a sign,
how I'd be shaken – wondering whether it
or the colours were being blown apart.
(As in a station, sitting in a carriage,
it seems we move when other trains depart.)

But listen – a small coincidence – a slam
from the hall (the curtains shook) and I am
less rational, more alone, since in my book
not seeing is believing. Hauntings?
Just the hustling wind and a far door bangs
and bangs. So who's unhinged? No snubbed ghost
  leaving,
no footfall creaks a plank but my own.

All eerie junketings, tall stories of
spooks grieving, the sounds of dread, can go hang
– and this room, too, quiet as language of the roses
or moss upon a wall. I hear nothing
when I hold my breath to hear it breathing.
Instead, from the courtyard, the bounce bounce
of a football and I feel comforted.

In my fashion

Dear, they said that woman resembled you.
Was that why I went with her, flirted with her,
raised my right hand to her left breast
till I heard the still sad music of humanity?
I complimented you! Why do you object?

Still you shrill, discover everything untrue:
your doppelgänger does not own your birthmarks,
cannot know our blurred nights together.
That music was cheap – a tune on a comb at best,
harsh and grating. Yes, you chasten me

and subdue. Well, that woman was contraband
and compared with you mere counterfeit.
Snow on the apple tree is not apple blossom –
all her colours wrong, approximate,
as in a reproduction of a masterpiece.

Last words

Splendidly, Shakespeare's heroes,
Shakespeare's heroines, once the spotlight's on,
enact every night, with such grace, their verbose deaths.
Then great plush curtains, then smiling resurrection
to applause – and never their good looks gone.

The last recorded words too
of real kings, real queens, all the famous dead,
are but pithy pretences, quotable fictions
composed by anonymous men decades later,
never with ready notebooks at the bed.

Most do not know who they are
when they die or where they are, country or town,
nor which hand on their brow. Some clapped-out actor may
imagine distant clapping, bow, but no real queen
will sigh, 'Give me my robe, put on my crown.'

Death scenes not life-enhancing,
death scenes not beautiful nor with breeding;
yet bravo Sydney Carton, bravo Duc de Chavost
who, euphoric beside the guillotine, turned down
the corner of the page he was reading.

And how would I wish to go?
Not as in opera – that would offend –
nor like a blue-eyed cowboy shot and short of words,
but finger-tapping still our private morse, '. . . love you,'
before the last flowers and flies descend.

Joke

While Freud was tracing the river to its source
he met Itzig unsteadily riding.
'Where are you going?' he asked that wild-eyed rider.
'Don't ask me,' said Itzig. 'Ask the bloody horse.'

Flowers

For the summer, I had prepared myself for the summer,
planted summer flowers to welcome friends in my
garden.
I hoped for such a display of colour in the summer.

Into my garden a statue trespassed into my garden.
A dream! Crazed, he ordered me to turn the black
earth over,
saying only black flowers would ever grow in my
garden.

Now summer has come and not one black flower has
come
out of the stone-repudiated earth of my garden –
not one flower so much in mourning that friends will
not come.

And yet, beloved, are these but funeral flowers in my
garden?
Their colours disguising grief that visitors cannot see?
At midnight, candidly black flowers in my garden?

Phew!

Do you know that Sumerian proverb
'A man's wife is his destiny'?
But supposing you'd been here,
this most strange of meeting places,
5000 years too early? Or me,
a fraction of a century too late?
No angel with SF wings
would have beckoned,
'This way, madam, this way, sir.'

Have you ever, at a beach,
aimed one small pebble
at another, thrown high, higher?

And though what ends
happily
is never the end,
and though the secret is
there's another secret always,

because this, because that,
because on high the Blessèd
were playing ring-a-ring-o'-roses,
because millions of miles below,
during the Rasoumovsky,
the cellist, pizzicati,
played a comic, wrong note,
you looked to the right, luckily,
I looked to the left, luckily.

Music

Music in the beginning, before the word,
  voyaging of the spheres, their falling transport.
Like phoenix utterance, what Pythagoras heard;
  first hallucinogen, ritual's afterthought.

A place on no map. Hubbub behind high walls
  of Heaven – its bugged secrets filtering out:
numinous hauntings; sacerdotal mating-calls;
  decorous deliriums; an angel's shout.

If God's propaganda, then Devil's disgust,
  plainchant or symphony, carol or fugue;
King Saul's solace, St Cecilia's drug;
  silence's hiding-place – like sunbeams' dust.

Sorrow's aggrandizements more plangent than
    sweet;
  the soul made audible, Time's other beat.

A scream

That scream from the street erased all content,
that uninspired cry of lunacy
left a vacuum. The ears of our cat

like clown-hats lifted. And silence extended
till this room, at midnight, resumed with one
manic bluebottle tap-tapping the lampshade.

Then you, brave, concerned, pulled the curtains
back.
We saw only the emptiness of our street
in lamplight. No blind hunter stumbled by

four times the size of a man. So many
enigmas! That night I dreamt we opened
the little wooden boxes of spikenard,

frankincense, cinnamon, saffron and myrrh;
also that herb from which can rise the antique
S-shaped, slate-coloured smoke to Paradise.

Ceilings

Sleepless, on the bed supine, I wonder
what cranky tenant left this ceiling scorched?
He must have been a giant with a flat iron.
Once, seemingly benign, another ceiling,
fifty shuffled years ago. Under it,
my mother taught me my name,
my father taught me the time.

Past bed-time though, poltergeists hurled lights
        outside,
caused cracks and stains to crawl, go wild, shake
        loose,
and fall malignantly beside a child
who half-awake, half beneath the bedclothes cried.
The alarm-clock hopped around the room surprised,
    flowers of the wallpaper
    poured forth illicit perfume.

The horror and the fragrance! Even at home
one may become an astonished tourist.
Listen: the oracle and the scalpelled
shadow, mumblings on the landing, almost heard.
Still emissaries from the other world
    seem near but not quite manifest,
    nag the mind like a mislaid word.

A grown man, though, should not rest so menaced,
so two-eyed, in the slow-pacing cuckoo night
of mid-summer, under a whipped ceiling,
to stare and stare again, suspiciously,
as in a zoo, at each primordial
    four-legged stain and serpent-crack
    as now I absurdly do.

Horse

You can't quite
identify it
the long straight road
unsignposted
zipping between hedges
to a scandalously
gorgeous sunset.
As you look closer
shading your eyes
with your right hand
vigilant you'll see
the visitant
the white horse
half way down it.

Do you remember?
Your father drove the car
the family squabbling
this way years ago
many a time
this Roman road
that's empty now
but for the distant
truant pink horse
with a barely
visible
red shadow
racing towards
the signals of sunset.

War-high in the sky
vapour trails fatten
and you know again
the common sense
of *déjà vu*. Perhaps
someone far from home
should be playing
a mouth organ
a melody slow
and sad and wanton
a tune you've heard
but can't quite say
as the purple horse
surprises the sunset.

And you close your eyes
trying to name it all.
But you recall only
the day's small prose
certain queachy things
what the office said
what the office did
as the sunset goes
as the black horse goes
into the darkness.
And you forget
how from the skin
below your thumbnail
your own moon rises.

Hotel nights

In the Angel Hotel

In the Angel Hotel no images allowed,
no idols. Artists, leave before midnight!

Do not strike a match in the dark laboratories
of Sleep where tomorrows are programmed.

Do not dream of stone shapes or listen to stone's
unauthorized version of silence.

Names have destinies. Write your own. Do not forge
a known sculptor's in Sleep's Visiting Book.

Else boulders will crash down. Like wood, malice of
stone:
wood once took revenge on a carpenter's son.

Now read the instructions in the event of fire.
Note the nearest exit door. Sleep well.

In the Royal Hotel

Should you wake in the dead middle of night
to skirt-like shufflings, unearthly laughter

in the next room, pipes insistently knocking;
should there be a mouse on the next pillow,

large as a frog, or should there be a frog,
do not telephone the old night-porter.

He needs his sleep, too. Instead recall
Sheba's meeting with the king, how she journeyed

years to hear Solomon's reputed wisdom;
how she sojourned in tents without air-conditioning,

without those other extras this hotel provides –
colour TV, Radio 2, herb-foam bath fluids, etc. –

how she arrived, at last, to record his first wise
  words,
changed into her jewelled apparel, unaware

three glass walls surrounded his golden throne;
how she thought the reflections to be water,

raised her skirts daintily, regally approached.
Then the great king uttered, 'You have hairy legs.'

In the Holiday Inn

After the party I returned to the hotel.
The room was too hot so I took off my coat.

It was January but I turned down the thermostat.
I took off my shirt but I was still too hot.

I opened the window, it was snowing outside.
Despite all this the air began to simmer.

The room had a pyrexia of unknown origin.
I took off my trousers, I took off my shorts.

This room was a cauldron, this room was tropical.
On the wall, the picture of willows changed

to palm trees. In the mirror I could see the desert.
I stood naked in my socks and juggled

with pomegranates. I offered offerings
that soon became burnt. This was some holiday.

I took off one sock and read the bible.
They were cremating idols, sacrificing oxen.

I could feel the heat of their fiery furnace.
I could hear those pyromaniacs chanting.

I could smell the singed wings of cherubim.
I took off the other sock and began to dance.

Like sand the carpet scalded my twinkling feet.
Steam was coming out of both my ears.

I was King David dancing before the Lord.
Outside it was snowing but inside it was Israel.

I danced six cubits this way, six cubits that.
Now at dawn I'm hotter than the spices of Sheba.

What shall I do? I shall ask my wise son,
Solomon. Where are you Solomon?

You are not yet born, you do not know
how wise you are or that I'm your father

and that I'm dancing and dancing.

Crepuscolo

Crepuscolo (Evening) is one of the partly finished statues by Michelangelo in the Medici Chapel, San Lorenzo.

To the grey Sacristy of San Lorenzo
tourists come whispering lest they waken
this self-absorbed statue and it assail
each prying one of them, lest a stone hand
uplift to point and the stone head utter,
slowly turning, 'Wrongdoing and shame prevail!'

Once all drowsy in Carrara. Harmlessly,
unnumbered shadows brooded under the weight
of rock-ledges, lizards hardly animate.
Then certain men came. Still the stone's cry
safe and soundless, still the statue slumbered
in the refuge of the rock's estate.

But, soon, massive slabs were brutally urged
from the mountain – the half-bright, half-stripped
  bodies
of workmen struggling in dazzle and bone-
white powder of marble, smoking sunlight.
How could they discern the one waking there
or hear stone words in the larynx of the stone?

And later, in Florence? Only the sculptor
heard the statue, almost delivered, crying
'Dear to me is sleep, dearer to be at peace,
in stone, while wrongdoing and shame prevail.
Not to see, not to know, would be a great blessing.'
So the statue pleaded, so the sculptor ceased.

More than four hundred years since they set out
from Carrara, each mile cursed and supervised.
The body in the rock staying young but the hair
turning grey and the face ageing utterly –
its idioplasm fixed, its night-accepting look
despairingly defined in the eyes not there.

Now, this evening, on exercise, three warplanes
dive on Carrara, flee, return, rehearse
radioactive speeds so shamelessly
that, in the x-rayed mountain, another
fifty million statues cower, unhatched,
and not one, stone-enslaved, wanting to be free.

AWOL

Did that spy, that wax golem
in Madame Tussaud's, blink?
Above inverted Kew Bridge
which semblant swan hid
both its beaky heads
under water like a fugitive?

Abruptly tipped off by MI5,
what spirits vacated the fountains
of Trafalgar Square, quit
the fussy trees in Hyde Park?
Who, in Harley St, requested
a prescription for ambrosia?

To answer – Sssh! Sssh! –
is to listen for bare feet
traversing the carpet of a hall;
to hear, in an evening room,
one small needle wakening
a Schubert piano sonata.

Listen, you semiologists!
It's the code of nightfall:
some lit windows, some dark;
fingers without fingerprints;
palms unlined. Forgery
in the sky, fire in the garden.

As if the Dii Majores joked
he was somewhere in London,
one of the sempiternal
30,000, unknown gods
who, after the annual feast,
visibly disappeared: smoke.

Millie's date

With sedative voices we joke and spar
as white coats struggle around her bed.
Millie's 102, all skull; once her head
was lovely – eyes serious, lips ready to be kissed
at Brixham, in 'the County of Heaven'.
She's outlived three wars and three husbands.
Her only child 'passed over', aged 77.

Sometimes she plucks the life-line in her small
left hand; remarks, 'An itch means money.'
Mostly, though, she's glum or incontinent
with memories. But now, like that immortal
of Cumae who hung in a jar, she cries,
'Let me die, let me die,' – silencing us.
How should we reply? With unfunny science?

Or, 'Not to worry – the Angels of Death
survive forever'? Often I've wondered
if some are disguised as vagrants, assigned
to each of us and programmed to arrive
punctually for their seedy appointments.
So where's Millie's escort, in which doss-house?
Has he lost his way, has he lost his mind?

Millie's quiet now, in a valium doze,
and window by window the building darkens
as lights go home. Outside, I half-expect
a doss-house beggar with a violin
to play, 'Ah, sweet mystery of Life' – some song
like that. Then any passer-by could drop
two coins, as big as eyes, inside his hat.

Case history

'Most Welshmen are worthless,
an inferior breed, doctor.'
He did not know I was Welsh.
Then he praised the architects
of the German death-camps –
did not know I was a Jew.
He called liberals, 'White blacks',
and continued to invent curses.

When I palpated his liver
I felt the soft liver of Goering;
when I lifted my stethoscope
I heard the heartbeats of Himmler;
when I read his encephalograph
I thought, *'Sieg heil, mein Führer.'*

In the clinic's dispensary
red berry of black bryony,
cowbane, deadly nightshade, deathcap.
Yet I prescribed for him
as if he were my brother.

Later that night I must have slept
on my arm: momentarily
my right hand lost its cunning.

The sacred disease

In another century, a wide-eyed priest
would be at Mr Kramer's ear: 'Gaspar
bears the myrrh, Melchior the frankincense,
Balthazar the gold. Go, spirit, depart.'
Else some old quack, a colleague in my art,
would prescribe blood of a red-haired woman,
young vulture's brain, young cormorant's heart.

When God entered Paradise, all the trees
burst into hymns; but here, on earth, demons
thrived, some unquiet, trapped in skulls. How odd
Guainerius's advice: 'Doctor of brainstorm,
or of dancing mania, should you see
your wincing patient fall, then urinate
in your shoe and let him drink it while it's warm.'

Greeks with Falling Sickness were less possessed
by demons than by gods. And what of
Saul's aura, Paul's faint? I think Kramer screamed
as loud, gnashed his teeth, rolled his eyes alight,
heavenward – like any agitated saint.
Comes night, they say, most epileptics pray.
Well, once, black fire wrote aleph on the white.

Today, the Supernatural's been converted
(and all its staff) into electrical
discharges. Read the encephalograph!
Mr Kramer, though, rises now dismayed.
Whom did he visit? He feels his skull with care
as if to find it trephined, some hole there
primeval, the secret spirit betrayed.

Tuberculosis

Not wishing to pronounce the taboo word
I used to write, 'Acid-fast organisms.'
Earlier physicians noted with a quill,
'The animalcules generate their own kind
and kill.' Some lied. Or murmured, 'Phthisis,
King's Evil, Consumption, Koch's Disease.'
But friend of student days, John Roberts, clowned,
'TB I've got. You know what TB signifies?
Totally buggered.' He laughed. His sister cried.
The music of sound is the sound of music.

And what of that other medical student,
that other John, coughing up redness on
a white sheet? 'Bring me the candle, Brown.
That is arterial blood, I cannot be deceived
in that colour. It is my death warrant.'
The cruelty of Diseases! This one, too.
For three centuries, in London, the slow, sad bell.
Helplessly, wide-eyed, one in five died of it.
Doctors prescribed, 'Horse-riding, sir, ride and ride.'
Or diets, rest, mountain air, sea-voyages.

Today, an x-ray on this oblong light
clear that was not clear. No pneumothorax,
no deforming thoracoplasty. No flaw.
The patient nods, accepts it as his right
and is right. Later, alone, I, questing for
old case-histories, open the tight desk-drawer
to smell again Schiller's rotten apples.

In the old age home where he says he's resting

he tree-watches, this autumn, zany Prospero,
ex-stage magician, old star of the lost Empires,
at the window, his powdered face perfect gallows.

Look our own eidolon! Between daft paragraphs
he hums 'Daisy, Daisy,' chuckles mildewed jokes
and waits for condescending visitors to laugh.

Like that tree, his mind's half ruined. Again
  complains
but not of Caliban. 'Son, any child could tell
this place needs renovating, can't you smell the
  drains?'

Or grumbles: 'Any child could tell they steal my
  clothes;'
suspects the Superintendent's snazzy shirt is his
before switching off to a mouth-gaping doze,

to the bleak mechanism. How molesting it
always is, the last real act. Does Miranda neglect him
now he cannot summon music from the Pit?

Prospero snores on. Ariel is unconfined, free,
and any child could tell but none will tell the child,
'Tis magic, magic, that hath ravished thee.'

A salute on the way

(*To Peter Porter*)

In the Land of late Evening,
miles yet from the bus terminus
where the electric outskirts end
abruptly (far beyond, the Old
Management is about to mend
  the fused stars) I hear you laugh.
  A warm, democratic laugh.

But I remember your 'Alas'
when the needle played the 'sssh' of black
round and round the record's label.
Then the god's thesmothete decreed
(all his aces on the table)
  the game was over – your bill
  the cost of seriousness.

It seems you've often played the lead
in a tragedy translated
by a too cheerful Australian
where the hero, at home, bereaved,
alone and feeling alien,
  takes off unscripted glasses
  quietly, to rub his eyes.

Thus, in the Land of late Evening,
though I hear, now, your candid laugh
more generous than a bridegroom's,
I can guess how, afterwards, you,
like good St Peter, will resume
  the slightly-pained look of one
  about to be crucified

upside-down. Peter-come-lately,
it's your turn to complain of
a *Collected Poems*; of rust
in the morning pelvis; of teeth
touching; of colleagues become dust;
    and nothing to say except
    facts, cats, and thriving heartache,

or who pushed whom and which one fell
(that yellow stain *is* Humpty Dumpty)
so to hell with the Old Management's
jackal-headed, hired psychopomp
whispering of money unspent,
    out there, in the banked darkness:
    'Follow me, follow, follow.'

Friend, let's not hurry. Who believes
these days in a second edition?
May we, unremaindered, go slow,
shadows lengthening between lampposts
on leafy pavements, or on snow,
    to the very last lamppost
    in the Land of late Evening.

In The Pelican

As a car rushes beneath a railway bridge
and its radio suffers local amnesia
so I'm also afflicted excuse me is that
YOUR glass so sorry with sudden blanks for
  instance
I've forgotten her name so how can I phone her
look her up in the book though last time in April
when I drove her home February actually
she was an ace she really was I remembered
to remember a mnemonic that would help me
to remember and now I've forgotten THAT
except it had something to do with the colour
of her dress which matched absolutely spot on
the audacious violet colour of her eyes and
YES this should interest you I made the mnemonic
rhyme with one of the old songs the really old songs
like Stormy Weather only it wasn't Stormy
Weather it wasn't Everybody's Doing It
it wasn't Smoke Gets in Your Eyes not Lazybones
not Stardust not Shoe-shine Boy not Whispering
  Grass
not it's on the tip of my tongue or was it
Thanks for the Memory you know what's his name
used to sing it in tandem with anyway
she was SO desirable and hell I wish I'd
asked her sorry Freud would certainly say something
stupid about how I keep reaching for your glass

A welcome in the wolds

Superior people never make long visits.
Marianne Moore

First day, Welcome! Welcome! We even ask your pet centaur – such a sweetie – if he'd like a bed or a stable

WOULD YOU LIKE A BED OR A STABLE?

First week, we offer you a symphony for a song, a garden for a daisy. We live to give. You wake to take.

Second week, we are *exhausted* with giving. Breakfast lunch tea dinner. So much shopping, so much cooking, so much serving and clearing up. So a treat, perhaps, at our favourite restaurant?

Your centaur eats like a horse. You *almost* insist on paying.

This is the beginning of But. This is the beginning of We don't mind. This is the beginning of Course not, silly.

Next day your centaur leaves our loo in one helluva spectacular mess.

Forget it, silly. Forget *it*.

And next week the conclusion of But. For the foisty centaur phones a friend on Mount Pindus, then one in the forests of Thessaly, then another in Famagusta and yet another in *Inner* Mongolia.

For hours.

Naturally he eats the last straw.

So you're for it sweetheart – you and your
phone-mad, full-bottomed, self-centred centaur.
Your finger for a fingernail, your eye for an
eyelash.

No matter, when you depart you're smiling, when
you depart we're smiling. Goodbye!
(In the hall, we pretend not to hear your centaur
farting.)
Goodbye!
Such a shame you both can't stay,
such a shame your pet must see
his Jungian Analyst.
Goodbye! Goodbye!

Now in the stable – renamed the Hercules Room –
a new sign: NO CENTAURS ALLOWED, NO
NEMEAN LIONS, NO LERNEAN HYDRA,
NO ARCADIAN STAGS, NO
ERYMANTHIAN BOARS, NO CRETAN
BULLS, NO CANNIBAL BIRDS, NO
THREE-HEADED DOGS, ETCETERA,
ETCETERA.

And in our guest-room a little card, beautifully
printed and framed on the wall: YOUR VISIT
GIVES US SO MUCH PLEASURE, IF NOT
YOUR ARRIVAL THEN YOUR
DEPARTURE.

A translation from the Martian

(For Craig Raine)

Who for the first time on earth saw the object that
earth-men call an and-mirror (sic)
who incognito picked it up who stared at it whose
eyes widened whose sixth toe curled up
who cried out delightedly
'Father. Father.'

Who hid it in his pocket who concealed the object
where his long-dead father lived
who occasionally gazed at it
who smiled at it sweetly who spoke to it softly
'Father. Father.'

Who returned home with it who kept his hand
upon his pocket who did not show the ghost to his
wife
who became suspicious who came close to smell
him who waited for his sixth toe to fall asleep who
stole the object from his pocket who secretly stared at
it who cried out scornfully
'Ach. It's only an old woman.'

Who took it to the window who watched it fall in
slow-motion who heard it clatter an hour later
on the red-hard rocks below
where the and-mirror (sic) broke into moonlight.

Pathetic fallacies

My dear one is mine as mirrors are lonely
W. H. Auden

Afternoon Mirror

So vain that mirror on the wall.
It waits there and waits there
just to be looked at.

Evening Mirror

Lonely, wishes another mirror
could be brought in, close by, opposite,
that it may reproduce itself.

Night-time Mirror

Suffers from nyctalopia, panics.
Depth charges to its surface. Sleepless,
prays to its own ghost, the window.

Morning Mirror

At last, at last, Visiting Hour.
The portrait gallery is open.
The Director does not seem pleased.

Quests

To reach the other world some sought hemlock
in waste-places: umbels of that small white flower
still sway at eye-level when the eye is still;

and some, at broad sunset, walked the sea-shore
or prayed for their messiah in a darkening house.
But gods had human faces and were flawed.

When prying Apion, with eerie conch,
summoned Homer's spirit to ask where he was born
whose bloody head appeared above the parapet?

Now at this seaport, in its shut museum,
a sculptured satyr on a sculptured sea-horse
blows only silent zeros through his horn.

And here, out of doors, more abundant silence.
Awesome over the sea, from which no sulking
Proteus
will rise, the candled stars, the unblinking moon.

Who knows? Not me. Secular, I'll never hear
the spheres, their perfect orchestra, or below,
with joy, old Triton playing out of tune.

The message

Found in the ruin
this urgent message:
I beg you, kindle
the fire I've prepared
in the secret forest.
Then say the old prayer.

But who can locate
that clandestine forest?
Under which tall tree
should the small fire blaze?
Besides, who can recall
the old words of the prayer?

No matter. Beautiful
the yellowing scroll,
its wild imperative,
its holy message,
that we shall keep safe
in safe or museum.

The vow

I dreamt or read on a yellowing page
how the wise one rode into Chezib's shade
  and a man shouted angrily,
  'Rabbi, nullify my vow!'

Didn't the sage turn to the man's companions
(some short, some tall, some grinning, some afraid)
    to cry, 'What? Is he drunk? Has he
    swallowed half a lug of wine?'

For three miles the man stumbled, zig-zagging
behind the ass, till the bearded one dismayed,
    dismounted, wrapped himself, sat
    with knees splayed on the dark grit.

Slow lessons of sunset. The man waited,
the ass waited also. The rabbi swayed
    with a ghost-wasp in his throat;
    at first star, nullified the vow.

This I recall from so many erasures.
Now dust falls on ledges, thousands of years fade;
    but listen, the crowds shout again.
    Look! The goggled outriders!

And behind the linked arms of policemen
I clutch, as beflagged cars cavalcade,
    a half lug of wine to wonder
    what was my vow, what was his vow?

The abandoned

There is no space unoccupied by
the Shekinah – Talmud

. . . thy absence doth excel
All distance known – George Herbert

I

God, when You came to our house
  we let You in. Hunted,
    we gave You succour,
      bandaged Your hands,
        bathed Your feet.

Wanting water we gave You wine.
Wanting bread we gave You meat.

Sometimes, God, You should recall
  we are Your hiding-place.
    Take away these hands
      and You would fall.

Outside, the afflicted pass.
  We only have to call.
    They would open You
      with crutch and glass.

Who else then could we betray
  if not You, the nearest?
    God, how You watch us
      and shrink away.

2

Dear God in the end you had to go.
Dismissing you, your absence made us sane.
We keep the bread and wine for show.

The white horse galloped across the snow,
melted, leaving no hoofmarks in the rain.
Dear God, in the end, you had to go.

The winds of war and derelictions blow,
howling across the radioactive plain.
We keep the bread and wine for show.

Sometimes what we do not know we know –
who can count the stars, call each one by name?
Dear God in the end you had to go.

Yet boarding the last ship out all sorrow
that grape is but grape and grain is grain.
We keep the bread and wine for show.

Soon night will be like feathers of the crow,
small lights upon the shore begin to wane.
Dear God in the end you had to go,
we keep the bread and wine for show.

Horizon

From these outskirts of Beersheba
a car moved away leaving a dream:
the surprise of a camel standing there.

At this garage, a bored camel beside
three dirty-coloured petrol pumps.
All day I wished I'd had a camera.

Suddenly, the camel's owner appeared,
solitary, melanous, centuries old.
Had he once climbed out of a corpse?

Proximate, the appalling and the appealing.
Even here, among flies, oil-drums, vacuum-
dust, advertisements, one of the 36?

The camel, disdainful, but scaled without fuss.
No word, no farewell. Half asleep I stayed
to watch them for miles becoming smaller, small.

Over the Negev, at last, the sun tired,
honey and thorns; still I could see
near the horizon, the suggestion of

a smudge moving. Which way? A return?
The apparelled rider on his camel
coming or going, going or coming?

Encounter at a greyhound bus station

If belief, like heaven, lies beyond the facts
what serpent flies with an ant between its teeth?

asked the over-bearded man with closed eyes.
Who are they who descend when they ascend?

this kabbalist with eyes closed, asked.
Are all men in disguise except those crying?

And what exists in a tree that doesn't exist,
its eggs looted by creatures not yet created?

★

Partial to paradoxes, disliking riddles,
I hummed and I hawed, I advocated

the secrets of lucidity. Then said,
Some talk in their sleep, very few sing.

Abruptly, the unwashed one opened his lids,
rattled one coin inside a tin.

I looked into the splendour of his eyes
and laid my hand upon my mouth.

★

Then he scoffed: You are like the deaf man
who knows nothing of music or of dance

yet blurts out, observing musicians play
and dancers dance – Stupid, how stupid

those who carve the air this way and that,
who blow out their cheeks and make them fat,

who mill about, clutch and maul each other
as if the very earth and all would fall.

*

And what could I, secular, say to that?
That I'm deaf to God but not in combat?

Cool pretensions of reason he'd dismiss
and if I threw stones he'd build a house.

Yet I begged: Dare to reveal, sir, not conceal;
not all, translucent, lose authority.

Fool, he replied, I'm empty, feed my tin,
which I did, of course, when the bus came in.

Exit

As my colleague prepares the syringe
(the drip flees its hour glass)
I feel the depression of Saul,
my mother's right hand grasping still,
her left hand suspiciously still,
and think – Shadow on the wall,
Nothing on the floor – of your
random, katabolic ways:

merciful sometimes, precise, but often
wild as delirium, or like a surgeon
with cataracts grievously unkind
as you are now, as you visit
this old lady – one beloved by me –
as you blunder and exit, moth-blind,
mistaking even the light
on mirrors for open windows;

and as my colleague prepares the syringe
I remember another butchering –
a botched suicide in a circumspect
bed-sitting room, a barely
discernible fake of a girl-corpse,
a marmoreal stillness perfect
except for the closed
plum-skin eyelids trembling;

and as my colleague prepares the syringe
I picture also a victim of war
near a road, a peasant left for dead,
conscious, black-tongued, long-agonized,
able to lift, as my mother can now,
at intervals, her troubled head.
And as my colleague drives the needle in
I want to know the meaning of this:

why the dark thalamus finally
can't be shut down when we sleep
with swift economy? Of that king
and his queen – David and Bathsheba –
the old parable is plain:
out of so much suffering
came forth the other child,
the wise child, the Solomon;

but what will spring from this
unredeemed, needless degradation,
this concentration camp for one?
My colleague forces the plunger down,
squeezes the temgesic out,
the fluid that will numb and stun.
'Shadow on the wall . . .' I call, 'Nothing
on the floor . . . Patron of the Arts!'

And as my colleague extracts the needle
from her vein, the temgesic acts
till the bruised exit's negotiated.
Then how victoriously
you hold the left passive hand
of the dummy in the bed
while I continue uselessly
to hold the other.

Last visit to 198 Cathedral Road

When, like a burglar, I entered after dark
the ground-floor flat, I don't know why I sat
in the dark, in my father's armchair,
or why, suddenly, with surgeon's pocket-torch
I hosed the objects of the living room
with its freakish light.

Living room, did I say? Dying room, rather.
So much dust, mother! Outraged, the awakened
empty fruit bowl; the four-legged table
in a fright; the vase that yawned hideously;
the pattern that ran up the curtain, took flight
to the long, wriggling, photophobic crack
in the ceiling.

Omnipotent, I returned them to the dark,
sat sightless in the room that was out
of breath and listened, that summer night,
to Nothing.

Not a fly the Z side of the windowpane,
not one, comforting, diminutive sound
when the silence calmed, became profound.

Friends

Since our acorn days we've been friends
  but now at this oak door
I sense you do not wish me well.
  Why so, I cannot tell.

Though red carpet and silver gong
  may welcome us within,
friend, be yourself. Give me your hand.
  Come, this is what we planned.

Bitter as coloquintida
  a green lampshade in the hall
turns the light on your face to bile.
  Friend, turn to me and smile.

I too have felt envy and rage,
    cursed this stranger or that;
with needles in wax, cast a spell,
    damned him or her to hell,

yet never a friend, no, not one
    I would still call a friend.
Now you whom I thought to be loyal
    wish me under the soil.

Apology

I have spoken so much lately
of death and of treachery,
better to have sung the forgotten
other song of Solomon.
Forgive me. I do not believe
the rainbow was invisible
till Noah saw it;
nor was I refreshed
by strange bread in the desert,
spring water in the desert.

The two drab tablets of stone
were two drab tablets of stone,
yet, beloved, this is my heritage;
also music of Solomon's song
on psaltery and dulcimer,
that which is lost but not lost –
like the beautiful rod of Aaron,
the beautiful rod of Aaron
first with its blossom
then with its ripe almonds.

Somewhere

Not because they'd chant a god up with spell,
daft bell, corybantic ceremony,
to hear him speak translated English, badly dubbed,
hardly synchronizing with his lips,

is there a closed room, somewhere, with polished
table, silver tray, glass of soap-bubbles
boiling over. Prettily, these bubbles float
in transparencies of cathedral silence.

They break on soundless objects, on chairs,
on hushed curtains, on ceiling, on walls.

Who wants one coloured bubble not to burst,
a door to open for its triumphant exit?

Carnal knowledge

I

You, student, whistling those elusive bits
of Schubert when phut, phut, phut, throbbed the sky
of London. Listen: the servo-engine cut
and the silence was not the desired silence
between the two movements of music. Then
Finale, the Aldwych echo of crunch
and the urgent ambulances loaded
with the fresh dead. You, young, whistled again,
entered King's, climbed the stone-murky steps
to the high and brilliant Dissecting Room
where nameless others, naked on the slabs,
reclined in disgraceful silences – twenty
amazing sculptures waiting to be vandalised.

2

You, corpse, I pried into your bloodless meat
without the morbid curiosity of Vesalius,
did not care that the great Galen was wrong,
Avicenna mistaken, that they had described
the approximate structure of pigs and monkeys
rather than the human body. With scalpel
I dug deep into your stale formaldehyde
unaware of Pope Boniface's decree
but, as instructed, violated you –
the reek of you in my eyes, my nostrils,
clothes, in the kisses of my girlfriends.
You, anonymous. Who were you, Mister?
Your thin mouth could not reply, 'Absent, sir,'
or utter with inquisitionary rage.
 Your neck exposed, muscles, nerves, vessels,
a mere coloured plate in some Anatomy Book;
your right hand, too, dissected, never belonged
it seemed to someone once shockingly alive,
never held surely, another hand in greeting
or tenderness, never clenched a fist in anger,
never took up a pen to sign an authentic name.
 You, dead man, Thing, each day, each week,
each month, you slowly decreasing Thing
visibly losing Divine proportions,
you residue, mere trunk of a man's body,
you, X, legless, armless, headless Thing
that I dissected so casually.
 Then went downstairs to drink wartime coffee.

3

When the hospital priest, Father Jerome,
remarked, 'The Devil made the lower parts
of a man's body, God the upper,'
I said, 'Father, it's the other way round.'
So, the Anatomy Course over, Jerome,
thanatologist, did not invite me
to the Special Service for the Twenty Dead,
did not say to me, 'Come for the relatives' sake.'
(Surprise, surprise, that they had relatives
those lifeless-size, innominate creatures.)

Other students accepted, joined in the fake chanting,
organ solemnity, cobwebbed theatre.
And that's all it would have been,
a ceremony propitious and routine,
an obligation forgotten soon enough
had not the strict priest with premeditated rage
called out the Register of the Twenty Dead –
each non-cephalic carcass gloatingly identified
with a local habitation and a name
till one by one, made culpable, the students cried.

4

I did not learn the name of my intimate,
the twentieth sculpture, the one next to the door.
No matter. Now all these years later
I know those twenty sculptures were but one,
the same one duplicated. You.
I hear not Father Jerome but St. Jerome cry,
'No, John will be John, Mary will be Mary,'
as if the dead would have ears to hear
the Register on Judgement Day.
   Look, on gravestones many names.
There should be one only. Yours.
No, not even one since you have no name.
In the newspapers' memorial columns
many names. A joke.
On the canvases of masterpieces
the same figure always in disguise. Yours.
Even in the portraits of the old anchorite
fingering a dry skull you are half concealed
lest onlookers should turn away blinded.
In certain music, too, with its sound of loss,
in that Schubert Quintet, for instance,
you are there in the Adagio,
playing the third cello that cannot be heard.
   You are there and there and there, nameless,
and here I am older by far and nearer,
perplexed, trying to recall what you looked like
before I dissected your face – you, threat,
molesting presence, and I in a white coat
your enemy, in a purple one, your nuncio,

writing this while a winter twig, not you,
scrapes, scrapes the windowpane.
  Soon I shall climb the stairs. Gratefully,
I shall wind up the usual clock at bedtime
(the steam vanishing from the bathroom mirror)
with my hand, my living hand.

1987–1988

Variations

The bad boy of the North-West coast

Before the grown-ups awake
and the wind blows out the stars
I'll rise and escape from home — haaya

I'll take clubs for the salmon
carved hooks for the halibut
I'll paddle the great canoe — haaya

At home they'll cry they'll miss me
I'll hunt for big-breasted girls
I'll give them boiled coloured sweets
and bracelets carved of goat horn
When I'm tall I'll bring them home — haaya

Then all my leering uncles
will wear their hats of spruce root
will drum and shake their rattles – haaya

But I'll thrash each one of them
I'll tear off my father's head-dress
I'll marry two girls at once – haaya

The smaller of the darlings
I'll dress in spotted sealskins
and earrings of abalone shell
the other with bigger breasts
shan't wear anything at all – haaya, haaya.

American Indian Song

The young man and the lion

(*For Tony Whittome*)

I

Such thirst, such afternoon heat!
First it would drink then it would eat.
It trod his head into a zwart-storm tree.
Silently
the young man wept.

The young man who had slept
beside the zwart-storm tree and who
                    on waking
in the oven of a lion's mouth
had feigned to be dead.

The lion licked the man's two eyes.
The man felt a stick
pierce that hollow in the back
                    of his neck.
So he turned his head a little.

He looked at the lion
                    steadfastly.
The lion thought, Is he alive?
And the young man guessing that
it thought he may be alive

settled, would not stir though the stick
sharply was piercing him;
                    would not stir
till the lion who first would drink
went three hills away to drink.

Dead, thought the lion. So it went
to drink water from the water.
And the man shifted. And the man ran
                    to leave meat-
odour in the zwart-storm tree.

2

'Help!' Zig-zag he ran, open-mouthed.
'Help! Hide me in a hartebeest skin,
save me!' we heard him shout.
'The lion that drank my tears
will surely seek me out.'

Under evening miles of coloured sky
roaring and roaring the lion came
to our village. It would not cease.
The mother of the young man cried,
'Oh kill the lion, kill the beast.'

We hunters raced from the huts,
vultures settled on a wall.
One-eyed we fattened our bows
and aimed at the cheated lion.
The lion was full of arrows.

Strange thing: the lion did not fall,
would not die. What was happening?
We aimed more arrows and some hurled
assagai. Still it would not bleed.
Its soul was in another world.

'Yes,' said the rattle man who knew best.
'That lion by a sorcerer
is charmed or else it would be dead.
Give up the man you're hiding
now the sun is round as blood.'

'No!' the mouth of the mother screamed.
'Not my son, no! I shall go instead.'
And arms outstretched ran out unarmed.
Later we tossed a white-eyed girl child
to the beast. She also was not harmed.

The lion wanted only that man
whose double tears it had drunk.
Roaring it woke the stars in the sky
– they came forth brightly one by one
to watch the lion that would not die.

From the hartebeest skin we pushed him out
and the lion swallowed its roar.
Bristling with arrows, with spears,
it trod the young man, it bit him.
It drank once more his double tears.

Now free to die the lion bled
through its hide blackly. In the dark
it died where the young man lay dead
on the ground. Far from the stars,
the dead man, the dead lion.

A Bushman Legend (Katkop dialect)

Lesson in reality (1)

If you see an evil man coming towards you and feel afraid,
make the sign of Shaddai, the sign of the Almighty, with
your right hand and cover your face with it.

Not one man but many
wherever I looked. Here. There.
In every city, every country,

my hand flew to my falling face –
middle fingers, a three-pronged *shin*,
my thumb bent to a *dalet*,
my little finger a crooked *yod*.
The sign of Shaddai.

I grew older:
my forehead spread massively,
my frightened right eye to the right,
my frightened left eye to the left,
and the palm of my hand now too small.

T. Carmi (Hebrew)

Lesson in reality (2)

They held up a stone.
I said, 'Stone.'
Smiling they said, 'Stone.'

They showed me a tree.
  I said, 'Tree.'
Smiling they said, 'Tree.'

They shed a man's blood.
  I said, 'Blood.'
Smiling they said, 'Paint.'

They shed a man's blood.
  I said, 'Blood.'
Smiling they said, 'Paint.'

Amir Gilboa (Hebrew)

100 hats

To balance one hundred hats on my head
100 hats   100 colours
a hundred hats a hundred colours and shades of
  colour
one hundred hats incandescent with colour

if there were one hundred hats on my head
how I would move with the crowd to the Square
and the people spread open like a fan for me
that I should throw up my hats in the air

if there were one hundred hats on my head
a hundred hats a hundred colours and shades of
colour
with the high sun glossing my hundred hats
with the high sun sparkling my hundred colours

how admiringly the people would say to me
100 people in 100 hats
'hooray' and 'goal' and 'well done' and 'hooray'
and jump with joy with each of my gay flying hats.

Amir Gilboa (Hebrew)

The merry-go-round at night

The roof turns, the brassy merry-go-round crashes
out music. Gaudy horses gallop tail to snout,
inhabit the phantasmagoria of light
substantial as smoke. Then each one vanishes.

Some pull carriages. Some children, frightened, hold
tight
the reins as they arrive and disappear
chased by a scarlet lion that seems to sneer
not snarl. And here's a unicorn painted white.

Look! From another world this strange, lit retinue.
A boy on a steer, whooping, loud as dynamite –
a sheriff, no doubt, though dressed in sailor-blue.
And here comes the unicorn painted white.

Faster! The children spellbound, the animals prance,
and this is happiness, this no-man's land
where nothing's forbidden. And hardly a glance
at parents who smile, who *think* they understand

as the scarlet lion leaps into the night
and here comes the unicorn painted white.

(*A variation of Rilke's 'Das Karussell'*)

Song for Pythagoras

White coat and purple coat
a sleeve from both he sews.
That white is always stained with blood,
that purple by the rose.

And phantom rose and blood most real
compose a hybrid style;
white coat and purple coat
few men can reconcile.

White coat and purple coat
  can each be worn in turn
but in the white a man will freeze
  and in the purple burn.